THE RENAISSANCE VINOY
ST. PETERSBURG'S CROWN JEWEL

BY PRUDY TAYLOR BOARD

THE
DONNING COMPANY
PUBLISHERS

Copyright © 1999 by Renaissance Vinoy Resort

The Donning Company/Publishers
184 Business Park Drive, Suite 106
Virginia Beach, VA 23462

Steve Mull, General Manager
B. L. Walton Jr., Project Director
Dawn V. Kofroth, Assistant General Manager
Sally Davis, Editor
Paul C. Gualdoni Jr., Graphic Designer
John Harrell, Imaging Artist
Teri S. Arnold, Director of Marketing

Library of Congress Cataloging-in-Publication Data

Board, Prudy Taylor, 1933–
    The Renaissance Vinoy : St. Petersburg's crown Jewel / by Prudy Taylor Board.
        p.   cm.
    Includes bibliographical references.
            ISBN 1–57864–087–3 (hc. : alk. paper)
    1. Renaissance Vinoy (St. Petersburg, Fla.)—History.
2. Renaissance Vinoy (St. Petersburg, Fla.)—History Pictorial works.   I. Renaissance Vinoy (St. Petersburg, Fla.) II. Title.
TX941.R45V56   1999
647.94759'6301—dc21   99–39917
                                                                      CIP

Printed in the United States of America

ENDSHEET: Guests of all ages enjoyed the wide sandy beach in front of the hotel, whether they swam or just strolled the shoreline searching for exotic shells or sharks teeth.

TITLE PAGE: For decades, the portecochere of the Renaissance Vinoy Resort welcomed the chauffeur-driven luxury cars of wealthy guests.

ABOVE: When it was time to select an artist to do the cover for the Vinoy history, Christopher Still, shown here with the Vinoy work in progress, was the first and only choice. There were a number of reasons. As a native Floridian, Still reveres both the state and its history. His skill is unquestionable, his vision unique. Previously, he was chosen by former Florida Governor Lawton Chiles' family to paint Chiles' official portrait, commissioned by the St. Petersburg City Council to paint two murals to be hung in city hall and had done a painting now in a private collection evocative of the sponging industry in Tarpon Springs where he lives and has his studio.

MORE BEAUTIFUL WITH TIME
A HISTORY OF THE RENAISSANCE VINOY RESORT

 T IS 1923 IN ST. PETERSBURG, FLORIDA. The son of a Pennsylvania oil baron, Aymer Vinoy Laughner, is negotiating a friendly wager with famous golf pro Walter Hagen. If Hagen can drive three golf balls off the face of Laughner's gold pocket watch without damaging it, Laughner will buy the property on Tampa Bay across from his home and build a resort hotel there. Hagen succeeds and moments later a contract is written up on a brown paper bag for the purchase of the Williamson homestead, a scenic twelve-acre site that in 1925 would open as the luxurious Vinoy Park Hotel.

Commissioned to celebrate the 75th anniversary of what is now the Renaissance Vinoy Resort, this oil painting by Florida artist Christopher M. Still reflects the hotel's interesting origins and rich history in myriad ways, while showcasing its Mediterranean Revival design and architecture. Seven different views of the building are depicted, along with the ornate dimensional frame, which is actually a combination of the hotel's entrance and its dining room window. The style and impeccable elegance of the bygone era shown here are still hallmarks of the resort today, following a $93 million, historically accurate restoration.

The numbered legend on the following page presents a more intimate look at what is behind some of the many interesting elements woven into the painting:

Oil Painting by Christopher M. Still—48" by 68"

1) Facade. This is the original ornate archway that towers over the front entry and still greets visitors today.

2) Thermometer. It rests on 75 degrees in honor of the 75th Anniversary. On cooler winter days the Vinoy doorman would artificially warm the thermometer to show the guests a more comfortable temperature.

3) Flowers. This arrangement was created by the former florist of the Vinoy, Lois Laughner Sullivan—wife of the founder's son. Tourists were impressed by orchids in the winter.

4) Corsage. The hotel guests always received an orchid from the manager when the winter season was over.

5) Dinner Ring. A tradition of formal dining in the 1920's, this particular ring belonged to the owner's wife—the great-grandmother of the young woman wearing it here.

6) Art Deco Playing Card. This design of the 1920's also shows the painting's composition and color scheme.

7) Frieze from Exterior Dining Room Window. The name of the hotel is carved in the ornate frieze that borders the original dining room window.

8) Paper Bag and Stock Certificate. The contract to buy the hotel's land was spontaneously drawn up on a paper bag following the golfing wager. The certificate was issued to investors of the future Vinoy Park Hotel.

9) Reflection on Vase. The blue vase reflects the artist in the hotel lobby as it looks today.

10) Chef's Fruit Plate. This special arrangement was created by the Vinoy's current garde manger chef.

11) Great-Granddaughter in 1920's Dress. Elice Laughner, the great-granddaughter of the hotel's original owner models a 1920's beaded "flapper" dress. Her father's name is Vinoy.

12) Bridge Hand/Playing Cards. Bridge, bingo and other social games were popular with guests who stayed throughout the winter months and spent great amounts of time together.

13) Marble. This is the marble used for the renovated check-in counters.

14) Oriental Carpet. Beautiful mosaic tile floors were covered with rich oriental carpets. The unique tile work still remains today as a focal point of the resort's lobby.

15) Tassel. A hotel detail found in early photographs.

16) Golf Ball and Club. The ball and club are the type used in 1925. The small "H" on the club identifies its owner, Walter Hagen, the famed golf pro who took part in the wager that determined the Vinoy Park Hotel would be built on the Williamson homestead.

17) Waiter's Pin. Waiters in the 1920's Vinoy dining room wore these identifying badges.

18) Original Room Key. During the resort's search for memorabilia, a St. Pete Beach resident returned this old Vinoy room key found on the local beach.

19) Pocket Watch and Chain. The Hamilton Railroad pocket watch, size 16, belonged to Perry O. Laughner and Aymer Laughner. It was part of the wager in which a golf ball was driven from its face into the land that became the Vinoy. The watch chain belongs to the present day general manager whose great-grandfather was a resident of St. Petersburg.

20) Matchbook. A picture of the Vinoy graces this matchbook cover from the period when Charles Alberding bought the hotel in 1945.

21) Clark Bar. The Clark family bought the Sunset Country Club, now known as the Vinoy Golf Club, where guests of the hotel have always played.

22) Coffee Cup. A picture of the Vinoy appears on this piece of hotel china from 1925.

23) Puzzle Pieces. A table in the lobby always had a puzzle in progress for guests to work on when passing. The pieces were made of wood.

24) Doorman's Jacket. The sleeve of a 1920's doorman's coat.

25) Silver Coffee Pot. From the original 1925 service.

26) Stenciled Pecky Cypress Beams. These beams are a unique detail of the lobby and survived the 18 years the hotel was closed.

27) Stucco Wall. The unique texture and salmon color of the building exterior. This special color is called Vinoy and is still used today.

28) Bride and Groom. Charles Fleet and Ruth Harvey, a newly wed couple, escorted their wedding party to the opening festivities of the Vinoy in 1925.

29) Fruit Arrangement. Fresh fruit baskets were always available for guests upon arrival.

30) Solarium. The solarium was a small private booth with an opening roof that allowed guests to sunbathe au natural. Children often climbed on the hotel roof hoping to catch a glimpse of the bathers. Small doors in the solarium permitted food and drink to be served discreetly.

31) Promenade Lobby. A place to see and be seen from the 1920's to present day.

32) Original Light Fixture. It is made of wrought iron and suspended by leather straps.

33) Tower with Electrician. The tower is a prominent feature of the hotel. Water was originally stored inside it to provide water pressure to the rooms, and local children often snuck into it to swim. The small figure of a young girl can be seen looking from inside the hotel. This image represents a story from the electrician's daughter—she feared for her father's safety as he installed lights in the tower for opening night in 1925. Red lights in the tower signaled the opening of the hotel and the start of tourist season. It now functions as a beacon and landmark on the downtown St. Petersburg waterfront.

34) Ballroom. Dancing was an important part of the social life of the hotel. The famous Paul Whiteman Orchestra was the Vinoy's house band.

35) Service Man, 1943-1944. The Vinoy was leased to the government as a cooks' and bakers' school for the Army Air Corps.

36) Sea Gull. A laughing gull symbolizes the hotel's Florida location on Tampa Bay.

OME YEARS AGO, WHEN THE BEAUTIFUL Vinoy was boarded up and closed, when she sat neglected like a spectre of years past, a shell, a blight even on St. Petersburg's waterfront, my late husband and I used to drive by when we were in town on various business errands. Because I grew up in hotels and feel more at home there than in most houses, I experienced a genuine sense of loss every time we passed her. In 1998 when I was approached to write the story of the hotel and share her fascinating history as well as the good news of her restoration and reopening, I was genuinely elated.

The elation never waned. Every visit was a pleasure and the more I learned of St. Petersburg's Crown Jewel, the more I appreciated both the hotel and her splendid staff. And so I say a very special thank you to Manager John Williams and his staff. Every waiter or waitress or bellman as well as the concierge staff and the people at the front desk were unfailingly polite, considerate and efficient. Public Relations Director Krista Boling and her assistants Elaine Normile, Amy Spencer, and Kelly Roberts went far out of their way to help me and they must share in the success of this book.

I also want to express my sincere gratitude to Craig McLaughlin, Tom Stovall, Dan Harvey, Anne Bland, Babe Fogarty, Bob Reynolds, Niles Laughner, Louise Berny Hamwey, Stephen Berny,

RIGHT: Broken windows, peeling paint, and overgrown foliage transformed the once elegant hotel. Its sad state of disrepair as caught in this photograph taken in 1977, evoked a sense of sadness in longtime St. Petersburg residents as well as visitors just passing by.

CONTENTS: The light in the Vinoy's tower signaled the opening of the social season.

FOREWORD: Yachts of wealthy guests such as the Guggenheims were docked at the resort for the entire season during the Renaissance Vinoy's early years.

8

Photo courtesy of ST. PETERSBURG TIMES

June Hurley Young, Betty Jean Miller, Mary Evertz, Mary Joan Mann, Pat West, Bobbi O'Malley, Lois Laughner Sullivan, Col. Harvey Sullivan, Hardy Bryan, Don Ivey at Heritage Village, Midge Laughlin at the St. Petersburg Museum of History, the Office of the Pinellas County Supervisor of Elections, Melissa Moore, David C. Beil, Frederick Beil, City Historical Preservation Officer John Hixenbaugh, Amelia Preston in the City Clerk's office, Norman Weyer, Kenneth Walden, Norman and Diane Bradford, Raymond and Kathy Arsenault, Hampton Dunn, and Eloise Shelton Cantrell. Without their generosity in sharing their time, their memorabilia and, most importantly, their memories, the book could not have been done.

And to my dear friend Esther Colcord a heartfelt word of thanks. Although we have coauthored a number of books together, for personal reasons she wasn't able to work with me on this one. Nonetheless, when I needed her help in making phone calls and doing research, she was there—as always.

Prudy Taylor Board
May 1999

CONTENTS

NATIONAL TRUST
for HISTORIC PRESERVATION

RICHARD MOE
PRESIDENT

FOREWORD

This book honors a legendary landmark whose commanding architectural presence, proud tradition of gracious hospitality and leading role in community cultural life and history have earned it the title of "crown jewel of St. Petersburg." Built in 1925 as the Vinoy Park Hotel, today's Renaissance Vinoy Resort is a living link with some of the most dramatic chapters of our nation's past – the Boom Era, the Great Depression, World War II and the good and bad times in between. In its 75-year history, the Vinoy has played host to thousands of business moguls, society leaders, celebrities and "ordinary" travelers. Happily, the high standards of comfort and service that made the hotel famous in its heyday are still alive today.

In addition to paying tribute to the Vinoy's founder and the people – famous and infamous – associated with the hotel over the years, this book tells an inspiring preservation success story. Like many other once-proud historic buildings, the Vinoy languished for many years, vacant and deteriorating, before visionary owners recognized its potential and returned it to its former glory. And, as has happened in dozens of similar instances across the country, the restoration of the Vinoy has helped to strengthen and revitalize the community that surrounds it.

Landmarks such as the Vinoy deserve our nation's attention and respect, as well as our best preservation efforts. They are eminently worth saving because they are irreplaceable. We are proud that the Renaissance Vinoy Resort is a member of the National Trust's Historic Hotels of America program, which was created to spotlight places like this – places that tell America's story, that enhance our quality of life, that offer unique traveling experiences by blending the best of yesterday and today.

As this handsome volume makes clear, the Vinoy has a proud past. More important, its spectacular restoration ensures that this outstanding Florida Gulf Coast resort will have a great future as well. That's cause for celebration among all Americans who care about their heritage.

Protecting the Irreplaceable

1785 MASSACHUSETTS AVENUE, NW · WASHINGTON, DC 20036
202.588.6105 · FAX: 202.588.6082 · WWW.NATIONALTRUST.ORG

A Glorious Beginning

THE YEAR WAS 1923 AND THE CHARMING, sun-drenched city of St. Petersburg was awash in optimism, opulence, and opportunity. The very air was alive with an almost frenzied rhythm of excitement. Fortunes were made overnight in real estate. A lot that sold for $500 on Monday resold on Tuesday for $1,300 and, by Friday, for $2,000. St. Petersburg's skyline changed from one day to the next as the construction industry followed in the wake of the real estate boom. Building permits skyrocketed in a mere three years. In 1920, they totaled $2.9 million and by 1923, reached $7.1 million. Bank deposits nearly tripled increasing from $5.9 million in 1920 to $16 million by the end of 1923.

The sidewalks bustled with crowds and the streets teemed with cars. "Tin can" tourists—visitors who had traveled south in their Model Ts, Reos, Buicks, and Packards—had either pitched tents or draped their cars with make-shift tarpaulins overflowing a campground near Lake Maggiore.

Wealthy tourists flocking south for the winter arrived by train to be met at the city's two stations by uniformed chauffeurs who had driven the family cars down. The roster included the superstars of industry and old money—the DuPonts, the Biddles of Philadelphia, the Guggenheims, the Fleischmanns, the Pillsburys, the Smiths of Smith-Corona typewriters, the Otises of the Otis Elevator Company, the Erbs of the Thom McCann Shoe Company, and the Clarks of the Clark Candy Company that made the Clark Bar and Teaberry gum. The city that Pennsylvania oil magnate Perry Laughner had chosen for his retirement in 1918 was truly booming.

Photo from the Renaissance Vinoy Resort Archives

PREVIOUS SPREAD: Memorabilia from another time surfaced during the Renaissance Vinoy's preparation for the celebration of its anniversary. Items featured here include a bellman's vest, postcards, blank stock certificates, and brochures.

ABOVE: Perry O. Laughner, founder of Laughner Enterprises, was born in Butler, Pennsylvania, on September 21, 1859. After attending business college, he went into the oil business where he was so successful as a broker, he went on to organize and operate several of his own oil companies. Following his retirement in 1918 in St. Petersburg, he and his son founded Laughner Enterprises investing in real estate. Their holdings included two thousand acres within the St. Petersburg city limits, the West Coast Inn, and several Beach Drive properties. He married Emma C. Finley on May 31, 1882. He and Mrs. Laughner had three children: Aymer Vinoy, Chalmers Clayton, and Gladys Marie who married Fred C. Beil. Perry O. Laughner died three months after The Vinoy Park Hotel opened.

RIGHT: These smiling realtors took part in St. Petersburg's annual Festival of States parade in the mid 1920s. They had a lot to smile about. Money was flowing freely and the living was easy. The Vinoy is in the background to the left.

16

Photo courtesy of Heritage Village

Actually, since retiring, Perry Laughner had had a change of heart. Along with his son, Aymer Vinoy Laughner, Perry had formed Laughner Enterprises to invest in various parcels of real estate in St. Petersburg. Not only had the Laughners entered enthusiastically into the business scene, they were no strangers in the city's social circles. Thus, on a night in early April 1923, Aymer Laughner and his wife, Stella, hosted a party at their home at 532 Beach Drive Northeast. The guests included Gene Elliott, the flamboyant and controversial developer who'd put together the financial package to build the Gandy Bridge, and professional golfer Walter Hagen.

What they did next was not unexpected given the fact that Hagen was world famous as a golfer. During his career, he won the British, American, North, South, Western, Canadian, and French Opens and, in 1927, led the American team to victory in the international competition for the Ryder Cup. It was about 3:00 AM. The three men were on the balcony. There, Hagen was hitting golf balls across the street off the face of Laughner's pocket watch. The other two had bet him that he couldn't do it without breaking the crystal.

Photo courtesy of P. T. Board

ABOVE: Walter Hagen was a phenomenal golfer. He won eleven major titles: two U.S. Opens, four British Opens, and five USPGA Championships including four in a row from 1924. He also won seven of his nine Ryder Cup contests.

LEFT: Aymer Vinoy Laughner, president of the Vinoy Park Hotel Company and the man who built the Vinoy, was a very savvy businessman who combined financial know-how with vision and foresight. Born in Oil City, Pennsylvania, on May 13, 1883, he went into the family oil business after graduating from high school and was eventually named president of Crescent Oil and Gas Company and Ma-Lou Oil Company, two of the family businesses in Pittsburgh. In St. Petersburg, he and his father, Perry O. Laughner, entered the field of real estate development. On June 3, 1908, he married Stella V. Watson. They adopted two children, Paul and Madalyn. In addition to his involvement in both the real estate and hotel businesses, he was elected and served on the St. Petersburg City Commission from 1930 until 1934. He died in 1961.

Photo from the Renaissance Vinoy Resort Archives

17

This house, the Aymer Vinoy Laughner home at 532 Beach Drive NE, was the scene of the momentous occasion in 1923 when Gene Elliott told Laughner they were going to build a hotel across the street and name it the Vinoy. It was from this porch that Laughner watched as his hotel was built across the street. Bought by Stella and Aymer in 1919, the four thousand-square-foot structure has six bedrooms, four and one-half baths, and was originally clapboard and frame. The home was sold to Joe Koon in 1978. A stucco contractor, Koon stuccoed the home.

OPPOSITE: This hand-colored postcard printed for the 1935–1936 season shows that a decade after its opening, The Vinoy Park still dominated the waterfront and the tower was still the tallest building. The back of the postcard accurately describes The Vinoy Park as "One of the Foremost Resort Hotels in America," and reveals not only that Clement Kennedy was still the managing director, but also that you could still send a postcard for a penny.

According to an interview with Aymer Laughner's son Paul, published in the ST. PETERSBURG TIMES in 1990, "Elliott looked toward the water and said to my dad, 'We're going to build a hotel there, and we're going to name it The Vinoy because that's such a pretty name.'"

Vinoy was, of course, Aymer Laughner's middle name. In the same interview, Paul Laughner explained his father's name came from a work of fiction about an Arabian chieftain. "My grandfather, Perry Laughner, loved books (novels) about men who were great fighters and great woman lovers. He found one whose name was Aymer Vinoy."

The next day as Laughner and Elliott crossed the street to retrieve their golf balls from the lawn of J. P. Williamson's home, Elliott, who actually never was involved in the hotel, suggested the Williamson homestead would be an ideal location since it was on the water. In an ensuing conversation with Williamson, they discussed Laughner's purchasing his homesite and Williamson agreed.

According to local lore, the agreement was scrawled on the back of a brown paper bag. However, these were the enlightened 1920s and everyone was very sophisticated about real estate transactions. As a result, a properly executed, witnessed, and notarized agreement dated April 9 was recorded on April 16, 1923. It conveyed Lots J, K, L, M, and N of Bay Shore subdivision from S. K. Williamson and her husband, J. P. Williamson, to A. V. Laughner for the sum of $170,000. Laughner, according to the agreement, paid $1,000 cash and agreed to pay an additional $5,000 within ninety days, $19,000 on or before February 1, 1924, and $145,000 on or before five years from the date of the agreement with interest at the rate of 7 percent per annum. Williamson levied additional conditions. The Vinoy had to surpass the three-hundred-room Soreno Hotel which had opened on January 1, 1924, and advertised itself as the city's first million-dollar hotel. The waterfront view had to be more spectacular than the Soreno's.

Vinoy Park Hotel   St. Petersburg, Florida

HAND-COLORED
POST CARD

Vinoy Park Hotel
St. Petersburg, Florida
One of the Foremost Resort Hotels
in America

Opens December 10th
for the Season of 1935-36

Clement Kennedy, Managing Director

* * *

Summer Resort—New Ocean House
Swampscott, Massachusetts

Mrs G. E. Handrick
45 Johnson Ave.
Binghamton
N. Y.

Courtesy of Elaine Normile

Competition with the Soreno aside, buying the property was the simple part. Two weeks after signing the agreement with the Williamsons, Aymer Laughner appeared before the St. Petersburg Board of City Commissioners to request an ordinance vacating Sixth Avenue Northeast of Beach Drive. The board agreed on the condition that a hotel be erected substantially as outlined by the hotel promoters, with the added provision that an outlet be given to Bayshore Drive on the northside of the proposed Vinoy Hotel.

In May of 1923, the city commissioners adopted a resolution requiring Laughner, in exchange for the ordinance vacating Sixth Avenue, to enter into an agreement providing that if he didn't construct and complete the hotel by May of 1926, he would deed the land on which he proposed to build the hotel to the city free and clear from any encumbrances.

Laughner had moved quickly because he was leaving for the summer, but once he was gone, progress slowed to a standstill. Action was still a rare commodity when he returned that fall. At a meeting of the city commissioners held on May 12, 1924, a year after signing the initial agreement, a letter from Laughner read into the record revealed that the city still had not moved to vacate Sixth Avenue.

An even more serious issue surfaced during that same meeting. In a separate letter, Laughner informed the city commissioners he had applied with the government for permission to fill the area in front of his land an additional eighteen hundred feet. This request was referred to a committee "with the power to act."

The clock was ticking, and months were passing. Two weeks later, the city commissioners adopted a resolution granting the vacation of Sixth Avenue, adding that Laughner had dedicated portions of Lot K and Sixth Avenue east of Beach Drive to "produce a more desirable ingress to the waterfront" and further that he had "by proper easement agreed to convey to the City for public street purposes one hundred feet across said property at or near its Eastern terminus…"

We will never know whether it was a bluff to force the city's hand, an act of frustration resulting from the fact that he felt stalemated, or simply a surrender to bureaucracy, but in the October 10, 1924 meeting of the city commission, a letter from Laughner indicated he was willing to sell the property to the city for $350,000.

The committee in charge of negotiating the purchase of Laughner's property reported they had had several conferences with Laughner and recommended that this offer be declined "as the price being more than we believe the City is justified in paying …"

In this photo by ST. PETERSBURG TIMES photographer John P. Jones, Hardy Bryan, Jr., holds Vinoy Park Hotel stock certificates dated March 12, 1925. A gift from his father, Bryan and his sister each received three shares of preferred and one of common stock valued at ten dollars a share.

Whatever Laughner's initial motivation, he finally won a significant victory at that meeting. Laughner was permitted to fill his property, but the amount of fill still had to be negotiated.

Negotiations, conferences, proposals, offers, and counter offers dragged on. In November of 1924, a compromise was at last reached. Laughner would fill twelve hundred feet instead of eighteen hundred feet, the land created by the fill would be leased to Laughner for five years provided he completed the hotel, and he could renew the lease for an additional twenty years with a reversion clause should the hotel ever be abandoned.

His battle with the city over, Laughner now turned his attention to the hotel's construction. In quick order, he had formed The Vinoy Park Hotel Company with a prestigious slate of officers and directors including Bayard S. Cook, former St. Petersburg city attorney; investment banker Robert B. Lassing; and bankers Amos P. Avery, T. A. Chancellor, and A. F. Thomasson. Also on board were Herman A. Dann of Dann-Gerow Building Supplies and Walter L. Wylie, M. D. Construction money was raised by selling $3.5 million shares of common and preferred stock. His next step was to hire local architect Henry A. Taylor to design the building and to contract with George A. Miller of Tampa to build it.

Miller gave Laughner his word that the building would be ready by December 31, 1925, an impressive feat since it gave him only eleven months to construct what was then one of the largest hotels on Florida's west coast.

The footings were poured on February 5, 1925, and the race to the deadline was on. By the end of the month, the TOURIST NEWS, a local news magazine, reported "Footings for all the wings of the hotel have been poured and forms for the massive pillars and walls are being erected. The concrete pouring tower, 120 feet high, has been completed and will be in operation as soon as the pouring of the walls begins."

The waterfront hummed with activity and Laughner wore a path through the hedge in the yard of his home on Beach Drive as he walked to the site daily keeping tabs on the progress. "Nearly five hundred men are now employed in the various construction and engineering phases of the work," the TOURIST NEWS continued. "More than one thousand men will be employed during the summer on the building of the hotel alone."

That August, reporter Ruth Crawford wrote in the TOURIST NEWS, "By day it seems a beehive of industry as huge derricks nois-

Photo from the Renaissance Vinoy Resort Archives

Henry L. Taylor, architect who designed The Vinoy Park Hotel, made significant contributions to the city of St. Petersburg. In addition to the Vinoy, he designed the Jungle Hotel (later used as the Admiral Farragut Academy); the Jungle Prada; St. Mary's and St. Paul's Churches; the Florida Theater (the first air-conditioned theater in St. Petersburg); the Adda Cadugan Building; and he was chairman of the group of architects which designed Jordan Park, St. Petersburg's first public housing. In 1940, he moved to Washington, D.C., where he worked for the Supervising Architect's Office, Bureau of Public Buildings. He died on December 29, 1958, in Arlington, Virginia, at the age of seventy-four.

ABOVE: George A. Miller, another native Pennsylvanian but a Tampa-based general contractor in 1923, had a reputation not only for doing quality work, but also for bringing projects in on time which is one reason Laughner chose him to build the Vinoy. Miller promised he'd complete the Vinoy in eleven months so the hotel could open December 31. 1925. He did better than that. He brought it in sixty days ahead of schedule. Miller also built the Soreno Hotel, the Belleview Biltmore near Clearwater, Florida, and the Tampa Citrus Exchange.

TOP LEFT: Actual construction of The Vinoy Park Hotel started on February 5, 1925. This photo taken fifteen days later indicates Miller wasted no time in getting the building under-way. By the end of February, he had nearly five hundred men on the job and the reinforced concrete footings were in place.

TOP RIGHT: Incredible progress is revealed by this photo taken six weeks later on March 16, 1925.

MIDDLE LEFT: On May 1, three months into the project, the hotel was taking recognizable shape.

MIDDLE RIGHT: The exterior walls had been completed and the tower was taking form a mere four months and ten days after the groundbreaking.

BOTTOM: When first completed in 1925, The Vinoy Park Hotel dominated not only the city, but the shoreline as well.

Photo from the Renaissance Vinoy Resort Archives

Photo from the Renaissance Vinoy Resort Archives

ily hoist the materials for finishing the exterior, while workmen go in and out putting the finishing touches on the interior. When night comes obliterating the unfinished appearance of the hotel, it is lighted only by one giant light on the observation tower and it becomes a palace—then St. Petersburg realizes that more than it ever hoped of, dreamed of has come true—it has the largest, most modern, and one of the most beautiful, fireproof hotels in the state of Florida."

The reporter rhapsodized over the hotel's beauty, but many of her visions became reality. "Can you not picture the hotel as it will be when winter brings the wealth of America to Florida?" she wrote. "Limousines driving up, depositing handsomely gowned women and men of affairs … How wonderful it will be to dance in that ballroom!… Then there is the tower! Whoever could resist the lure of a tower where one can climb to a world so different from the prosaic, work-a-day world we weary of sometimes?"

This was more than a progress report. It was an early expression of the respect and affection St. Petersburg's citizens felt for The Vinoy Park Hotel, an affection that would grow during the passing decades and eventually help save the Vinoy in the dark years that would lie ahead. But for now, it was the very best of times and the future looked bright and secure.

That same month, a new actor in the drama of the Vinoy's opening signed on—Karl Abbott, the hotel's first manager. In his book "Open For The Season," Abbott, a seasoned hotel man, described coming to St. Petersburg the first week of August 1924 and finding "a modern city with large office buildings and modern fireproof hotels. The traffic was heavy and the streets were lined with hundreds of real estate offices, some of which had barkers outside, like a sideshow, haranguing the passing crowds, 'Hurry, hurry, buy now!'"

Abbott checked into the Princess Martha Hotel and the next morning, looking through the window of his room, he saw "the steel frame of a structure built upon a sand spit that jutted out into the bay. It was painted with red lead and looked enormous."

Informed by the bellboy that this unfinished structure was the new Vinoy Park Hotel, Abbott got the address and, after breakfast, went to the office where he met Aymer Laughner and the other directors and told them he "had come down to operate their new hotel."

Impressed by Abbott's background and experience, as well as his brash confidence, Laughner hired him the following day.

Photo from the Renaissance Vinoy Resort Archives

Karl Abbott, first managing director of The Vinoy Park Hotel, was one of the country's leading hotel men. Born in Bethlehem, New Hampshire, on April 12, 1889, he graduated from Tufts College in Massachusetts and did two years of postgraduate work at the Wharton School of Business in Philadelphia, Pennsylvania. In 1910, he came to Florida as front desk clerk at the Alcazar Hotel in St. Augustine, Florida, and worked the following year as room clerk at the Royal Palm Hotel in Fort Myers, Florida. His success there secured for him the post of manager of the Gasparilla Inn in Boca Grande, Florida. He also served as manager of the Forest Hills Hotel, in Franconia, New Hampshire; The Kirkwood in Camden, South Carolina; and The Vendome in Boston, Massachusetts.

Abbott faced a daunting task. He now had five months to equip and furnish the hotel. One of his first acts was to travel to the Commodore Hotel in New York City where he rented nearly an entire floor. He had the furniture removed from many of the bedrooms and then arranged with a number of manufacturers to bring their merchandise and wares and set up displays in the now empty rooms.

It was a madhouse. According to Abbott, there were furniture people, carpet people, silver people, china and linen, and blanket people. There were representatives from kitchen equipment companies, printing equipment companies, draperies, elevators, lawn furniture, firefighting equipment, piano and organ people, refrigerating people, safe and vault people, office fixture people, bar fixture people, lamp and lampshade people, plumbing fixture people, venetian blind people—each vying for attention, each trying to "close the deal."

To add to the challenge, he writes, "… there was an embargo on all building material, equipment, and furniture into the state of Florida. Freight cars were backed up on sidings miles into the country." Materials had to be brought in by boat which meant that at times more than twenty freighters were docked for unloading in the harbor.

Construction continued through summer and early fall although, as Paul Laughner revealed later in an interview with a St. Petersburg Times reporter, "the man doing the hotel had to ask the

LEFT: The Vinoy Park Hotel china was designed by one of the country's foremost artists in this type of work, Koch of the Onandaga Pottery of Syracuse, New York. Service plates, similar to the one shown here, featured a colorful design that covered the entire plate and included a depiction of the hotel along with motifs of mermaids, palm trees, sea birds, seaweed, sea shells, dancing waves, puffball clouds, and smaller tropical scenes.

RIGHT: The silver service chosen for the Vinoy was made by the International Silver Company of Meriden, Connecticut, and consisted of 4,057 pieces of hollowware and 14,152 pieces of flatware. The flatware pattern was Paisley and of the Georgian period. Much of the Vinoy's silver was either sold during an auction in the 1970s or vanished during the hotel's lean years. Most of these items were either found in a vault discovered in 1992 when the hotel was being restored or returned by longtime residents who kept them safe, hoping—even in the hotel's darkest hours—that someday the Vinoy would reopen. One little cream pitcher carries a charming story. Years ago, Mae Risher was attending an affair at the Vinoy. She left her little dog in the car and went inside to ask a waiter for some cool water for the puppy. The waiter, trained to provide the ultimate in service, obliged and brought her the water in the little cream pitcher. She'd forgotten all about it until she read the Renaissance Vinoy was preparing to observe its anniversary and was asking for memorabilia.

Photo from the Renaissance Vinoy Resort Archives

Photo from the Renaissance Vinoy Resort Archives

fill people how much land he'd have to build on the next day." As it turned out, Miller brought the hotel in sixty days ahead of schedule which was just as well since reservations had been pouring in.

When the construction dust settled, St. Petersburg's crown jewel soared seven stories skyward. Of Mediterranean-Revival design, The Vinoy Park Hotel was one of Henry L. Taylor's finest designs and everything Aymer Vinoy Laughner had dreamed and planned. It was described in the souvenir booklet published to mark its opening as the "most beautiful and imposing structure" on the West Coast of Florida.

Among its dramatic and striking architectural features were its octagonal observation tower and the entrance loggia. Adorned with stone columns and ornamental panels, the loggia's floor was of quarried stone. The door was embellished overhead with the Vinoy crest, a *fleur de lis* and crown held aloft by two cherubs.

Photo from the Renaissance Vinoy Resort Archives

LEFT: This photo of the southern wing that also appeared in THE ARCHITECTURAL FORUM emphasizes the tower which was the tallest structure of its day. An intimate dining room was housed in the octagon-shaped tower and used for private parties. Although the tower is now closed to guests, it remains a cherished landmark.

OPPOSITE
TOP: The wicker chairs on the loggia were comfortable, the view spectacular, and the company compatible so it was a splendid place to meet friends and chat.

BOTTOM: The spacious lobby of The Vinoy Park was masterfully designed to take maximum advantage of natural light. The floor was of glazed quarry tile. The stenciled pecky cypress beams added to the Mediterranean influence as did the stunning light fixtures. Shown here in the foreground, the fixtures were suspended by hand-tooled leather straps which created a flat effect and gave the appearance of huge beams.

The lobby, which ran parallel to the entrance loggia, was stunning with its arched, two-story high vaulted ceiling and its glazed quarry tile floor. Divided into three sections, it contained a flower shop, a candy shop and cigar booth managed by the hotel, an area where guests could send telegraphs, and a bank of telephones along with the front desk.

The elegant entrance was enhanced by the impressive stonework designed by Henry F. Taylor, hotel architect, and constructed of Florida limestone by A. J. Arnold of the Ornamental Stone Company of St. Petersburg. Arnold invented a process which fortified natural rock. Surmounting the carved stone treatment, the twisted stone columns and ornamental panels, was a stone replica of the Vinoy crest which features a *fleur-de-lis* and a crown upheld by two cherubs. Reportedly, this was the crest of the French House of Vinoy.

Photo from the Renaissance Vinoy Resort Archives

Just beyond the lobby was the Palm Room. As with the lobby, the Spanish influence was predominant and it was spectacular. As described in the souvenir booklet, the Palm Room had two fountains of ornamental stone placed in the center at each end of the room. They were surrounded by palms and ferns. Giving the room its name was the abundance of palms placed at frequent intervals on high pedestals. It was, according to the booklet, "carpeted in gray and green … the hardware is beautiful hand-hammered silver. The walls, as in the lobby, are antique plaster and the ceiling is beamed."

The color scheme was completed in the furniture. Most of the tables and chairs were enameled French cane in orange and blue. Settees and glass-topped tables were of green enameled and decorated wood. Striped black moiré silk was placed beneath the glass tops. A note of whimsy was displayed in the lighting fixtures chosen. They were "in the semblance of cages with lights surrounding. Within each cage on a metal perch sits an unperturbed metal 'Polly,' finished in the gay colors of its animated model."

Photo from the Renaissance Vinoy Resort Archives

The Palm Room leads off the lobby into the ballroom. For years, the scene of the afternoon tea from 4:00 PM till 5:00 PM, the Palm Room was featured in the April 1928 edition of THE ARCHITECTURAL FORUM.

29

Photo from the Renaissance Vinoy Resort Archives

Photo from the Renaissance Vinoy Resort Archives

Photo from the Renaissance Vinoy Resort Archives

A Room of Sunrise and Moonlight

In his book, Abbott portrayed the ballroom as "one of the largest and most beautiful in Florida." It was two stories high, 50-feet wide and 125-feet long. The stage had a proscenium arch at one end and a cove that spanned three sides of the room with hundreds of colored lights hidden behind it, controlled by rheostats. The controls were in the wings of the stage and, he writes, "by manipulating these controls the room could be flooded with different-colored lights and spectacular effects, from sunrise to moonlight, could be achieved."

The dining room overlooked the bay and could easily accommodate seven hundred guests. The attention to detail was unmistakable here as was the vivid influence of ancient Pompeii. According to the souvenir booklet, "The walls are canvassed and painted in Pompeiian reds, blues and black. There are some forty panels in all, each different in design." The chairs, tables, and other furniture were enameled in the same shade of red and striped black. The window drapes were of a Pompeiian red satin as were the side curtains and festooned valance with a black and gold cornice.

LEFT: Ancient Pompeii with all its lavish beauty was the inspiration for the decor of the Vinoy's dining room.

OPPOSITE
TOP: The Vinoy Park ballroom.

BOTTOM: The imposing entrance to the ballroom as featured in THE ARCHITECTURAL FORUM.

For those guests wishing to dine more intimately, private dining rooms were located on the mezzanine floor which also contained a dining room for children.

The hotel contained 375 rooms and private baths. Each room was fifteen-by-fourteen feet in size and furnished with deep gray hair-wood furniture striped with a band of walnut. Draperies were of rose and green striped mohair. A sign of the times, the accoutrements in each room included an elegant, white porcelain, gold-banded spittoon. Connecting doors made it possible for guests to create suites or even guest wings. This was an especially attractive feature for the wealthy families who wintered at the Vinoy.

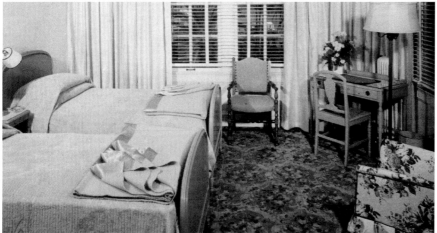

TOP: The mezzanine was a marvelous place to catch some rays, swing your troubles away, and watch boats plying the waters of Tampa Bay.

BOTTOM: A typical room at The Vinoy Park Hotel was fifteen-by-fourteen feet in size. Laughner deliberately kept the rooms rather small because he felt guests should not spend too much time in them. Each room had a modern, private bath, a roomy closet large enough to hold a steamer trunk and, when it first opened, an elegant decor highlighted by sienna walls and taupe velvet carpeting. The nightly rate was twenty dollars and included meals. At the time, The Vinoy Park was one of the most expensive hotels in the state.

33

RIGHT: The bell staff was formally attired in 1925 when the hotel first opened. The style of the uniforms would change over the years, but never surpass the elegance displayed in this early postcard.

OPPOSITE: At the grand opening, one of the highlights of the evening was the appearance of the Paul Whiteman Orchestra which provided music for dancing. Joe Lucas led the unit orchestra that evening but in later years Whiteman appeared in person at the Vinoy many times as did Guy Lombardo, Peter Duchin, and other famous bandleaders of the times. Dancing was always an important part of the season at the Vinoy and a house orchestra was employed each season to play for afternoon tea, for dinner, and for dancing later.

By December 31, 1925, the date of the grand opening, many seemingly unconquerable obstacles had been overcome. The hotel was completed, a thoroughly professional, carefully chosen staff was on hand, and the furnishings and linens had arrived. However, the day before the opening, the installation of the refrigeration system hadn't been completed. What was a party without ice? Abbott moved quickly and purchased ten tons of ice. But where do you store twenty thousand pounds of ice? Abbott and his crew solved that problem, too. The ice was stacked on the floor and along the walls of a store room in the basement. Cooks and their assistants found themselves slipping and sliding around the ice carrying huge pots of jellied soup and quarters of beef.

It was the final act of the drama and according to Abbott, "The last twenty-four hours (before the hotel opened) the dining-room and housekeeping crews worked straight through, setting up the dining room and guest rooms.

"Thirty thousand dollars' worth of linen had to be laundered and put on the shelves … The Vinoy was due to open for dinner at exactly seven o'clock in the evening. At five-thirty men were still laying

Postcard from the Renaissance Vinoy Resort Archives

the oriental rugs in the lobby and electricians were feverishly trying out the lighting system in the huge ballroom."

At six-thirty that night, every light in every room on the front of the building was turned on. At five minutes till seven, four doormen strode to the main entrance. They were impeccably groomed wearing black boots with white kid tops, white trousers, long powder blue coats, and tall silk hats with cockades. At precisely seven o'clock, they stepped forward and opened the doors.

Although the event merited only a couple of paragraphs in area newspapers, it was an impressive opening. Five hundred Shriners and their wives attended a banquet in the main ballroom. The main dining room was sold out and thirty-six dinner parties ranging from eight to forty people had been booked.

Romance was in the air, as well. That New Year's Eve, local socialite Ruth Harvey had married Charles Carvel Fleet in her home earlier in the evening. Following the ceremony, the newlyweds took the wedding party and their guests to the hotel to participate in the opening.

Invitations had been issued to several hundred of St. Petersburg's leading citizens including developer Perry Snell; newspaper owner L. C. Brown; George Gandy, Jr.; and Soreno Lund, son of the man whose Soreno Hotel had opened the previous year. The Laughner

Photo from the Renaissance Vinoy Resort Archives

35

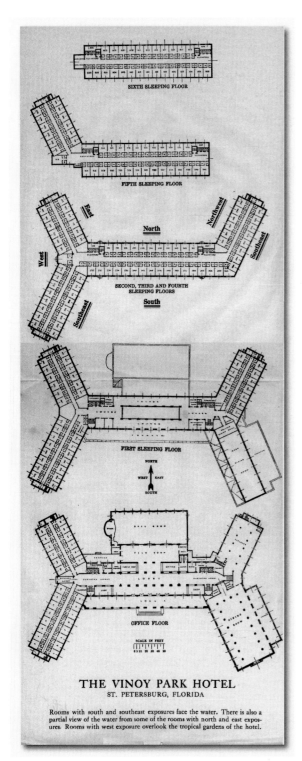

THE VINOY PARK HOTEL
ST. PETERSBURG, FLORIDA

Rooms with south and southeast exposures face the water. There is also a
partial view of the water from some of the rooms with north and east exposures. Rooms with west exposure overlook the tropical gardens of the hotel.

Photo from the Renaissance Vinoy Resort Archives

Photo courtesy of St. Petersburg Historical Museum

family was on hand with the exception of A. V. Laughner's sister, Marie Beil. She'd looked forward to attending and had
even ordered a gown from Paris for the gala event.
Unfortunately, her son had contracted scarlet fever and she had
to remain home with him.

But everyone else who was anyone was there.

After a splendid repast consisting of an array of gourmet delicacies including Essence of Chicken and Cold Roast Tongue
of Ox, the party adjourned to the ballroom. Aymer and Stella
Laughner led off the evening, dancing to Paul Whiteman's
orchestra conducted by Joseph Lucas. In later years, while The
Vinoy had its "house" orchestra for tea dances, dinner music,

OPPOSITE: This floor plan details The Vinoy Park Hotel as it appeared when it first opened. Every room was positioned to have a maximum view of either Tampa Bay or the beautifully landscaped tropical gardens.

LEFT: St. Petersburg was already a good-sized city when this aerial photo was taken on March 29, 1926. Looking northeast from the Methodist Church, the newly opened Vinoy Park Hotel is in the center background.

ABOVE: Howard Bland hired on as the Vinoy's first chief engineer and stayed on the job for nearly forty years, supervising not only the operation and maintenance of the up-to-the-minute steam heat system which he poses next to in this photograph, but also the overall upkeep of the hotel including the summer when it was closed for the season.

OVERLEAF: Open for the season. The finished hotel, one of the finest examples of Mediterranean-Revival architecture in Florida, rose proudly against the backdrop of Tampa Bay in this photo taken in early 1926. The hotel's construction was tested during the hurricane of 1926, but only the roof was damaged. Repairs cost $12,000 and were completed in ample time for the opening of the 1927 season.

and after dinner dancing, the ballroom hosted every major big band including Whiteman's orchestra which he later conducted personally, and Guy Lombardo.

And so The Vinoy Park Hotel's first season was launched successfully with a glittering affair guests would remember decades later. Rates were in the $15 to $20 per day range and included meals and business was brisk. The hotel closed for the season in April 1926, the guests went home, but the work wasn't over. The splendid edifice had to be tended and maintained. Chief engineer Howard Bland was the obvious choice.

Bland and his new bride, Anne, had taken jobs with the hotel just for the season, just to spend the winter in Florida. Mrs. Bland was one of the hotel's first four telephone operators. She remembers Laughner and Sterling Bottome, then working for Laughner in Laughner Enterprises, meeting with her husband, and convincing him to stay year round. It wasn't difficult because both she and her husband had grown to love the hotel in those few months. And so Bland stayed, year after year, caring for the hotel until his retirement in 1955.

"There was a lot to be done summers," Mrs. Bland remembers. "Howard and his men did a lot of painting and general maintenance. They took the carpets up for cleaning. And, of course, someone had to be there to get things organized when it was time to prepare for the reopening each Winter."

Financially, the hotel lost money that first season, but it proved to be more because of the start-up expense rather than the desperate economic problems confronting St. Petersburg and the rest of Florida. Statewide, the real estate market had collapsed under the weight of the inflated prices. Bank deposits plummeted and the building industry was in a serious slump. However, the wealthy families who stayed at the Vinoy were not effected and so the day-to-day operation of the Vinoy was untouched.

Furthermore, while the economic situation was not helped when a monstrous hurricane swept through Florida on September 19, 1926, killing nearly four hundred people, Laughner's confidence in

LEFT: To this day, St. Petersburg resident Norman Bradford (third musician from the right) recalls the thrill he and the other members of the YMCA band experienced the day this photo was taken at the Vinoy. They had just played for President Coolidge who was staying at the Vinoy during a brief visit. Bradford still remembers President Coolidge sitting on the veranda wearing his ever-present black fedora.

RIGHT: Among noted political figures who visited The Vinoy Park Hotel was President Calvin Coolidge. A man of simple tastes, hotel lore has it that he preferred to eat in the employees' cafeteria rather than sample the gourmet fare in the hotel's fine restaurants. Anne Bland remembers that while he was a very quiet, reserved guest and easy to please, the staff scurried on those rare occasions they were summoned to his suite.

Photo courtesy of Norman Bradford

builder George Miller proved to be well placed. The only damage was to the roof and that was quickly repaired.

Mrs. Bland remembers the hurricane only too well. "We were sitting in our living room in the hotel when that wind came roaring through, but we felt safe. The next day, Mr. Laughner said, 'Howard, you hire all the carpenters you can get' and he hired 28 carpenters to put on a temporary roof until they could make permanent repairs."

The second season opened in December of 1926 with a new manager, Clement Kennedy, and a $500,000 mortgage. Kennedy would turn the hotel around financially within a couple seasons and remain as manager until World War II when he would be called to serve in the U.S. Army Reserve.

The years of Kennedy's reign were exciting and eventful. The four-month season opened each December when the red light was turned on in the tower. For years, the turning on of that light signaled the beginning of the season in St. Petersburg. And each April, the hotel closed to doze through the languid, hot Florida summers.

Then as now, many famous people stayed at the Vinoy— the socialites, the wealthy families, but also former President Calvin Coolidge; Polar explorer Admiral Richard E. Byrd; writer, editor, and social critic H. L. Mencken; movie stars including James Stewart and comedian Edward Everett Horton. Stewart was so impressed he convinced his father to visit. The New York Yankees came to St. Petersburg for spring training and were housed there and, although

LEFT: Admiral Richard E. Byrd held the world rapt as word came that he and his pilot, Floyd Bennett, had reached the North Pole on May 9, 1926, a feat for which he later received the Medal of Honor. Although his claim was later disputed, Byrd made five expeditions to the Antarctic claiming an immense territory for the United States. He, too, was a popular visitor to the Vinoy.

MIDDLE: The Vinoy's roster of prominent guests included not only renowned novelist F. Scott Fitzgerald, but H. L. Mencken (shown here), arguably the most celebrated and respected newspaperman, essayist, book reviewer, and political commentator of his time.

RIGHT: Colorful baseball star Babe Ruth spent many of his twenty-two years in baseball at spring training camp in the St. Petersburg area and longtime Vinoy employee Anne Bland remembers he stayed at the hotel before leaving the New York Yankees in 1932. During one training session and while catching balls in the outfield, Ruth walked off the field declaring, "I ain't going out there anymore. There're alligators out there." Sure enough, alligators had emerged from the lake to see what was happening on their turf.

Photo courtesy of P. T. Board

Photo courtesy of P. T. Board

Photo courtesy of P. T. Board

the registers have long since vanished, Anne Bland remembers baseball superstar Babe Ruth staying at the Vinoy.

Business was good both for the hotel and for the very exclusive shops in the lobby. In a 1998 interview, Elaine Normile, the Vinoy's History Tour Coordinator, spoke with Louise Berny Hamwey and Stephen Berny about the shop their father, Michael Berny, had in the lobby where he sold linens and china imported from Europe. He operated the shop from 1928 until 1943, closed it during World War II, and then reopened it in 1946 and operated it until 1960 when he retired.

ABOVE: Taking in some sun at the Vinoy was winter guest Dr. John H. Willey of Montclair, New Jersey. Willey, an international figure in church circles and known as the "pulpit master" in Protestant church affairs, had just been appointed to the church board which supervised nineteen denominations. He was prelate of the Knight Templars Commandery and chaplain of the Sons of the American Revolution of New Jersey.

RIGHT: This aerial photograph of St. Petersburg taken from three thousand feet presents a fascinating portrait of St. Petersburg's waterfront in the late 1920s.

Photo from the Renaissance Vinoy Resort Archives

Mrs. Hamwey remembers that her father had a "handshake" contract with first Kennedy and then Bottome who succeeded Kennedy as managing director. The rent was $1,000 for the season and the "contract" included lunch served to him in his shop by a uniformed waiter.

Their routine was similar every year. Like many of the Vinoy employees, Berny had a shop summers at the New Ocean House in Swampscott, Massachusetts. In early December, he would drive to St. Petersburg, find a rental for his family and open the shop. His wife and children would arrive a few days before Christmas and return to their home in Boston by Easter.

Mrs. Hamwey remembers there was a jewelry shop across from his linen shop. Afternoon tea was served in the lobby, but the Bernys weren't allowed in the lobby because they were not guests, but shopkeepers. Steve, however, sometimes helped his father in the shop and had occasion to see the guests coming down for dinner.

"They were elegant," he said. "The men wore tuxedos, the women in evening gowns and never the same ones. They dined in the dining room, danced in the ballroom and afterward strolled down Bayshore Drive with their chauffeur-driven cars following behind."

The generosity and foibles of the very wealthy led to some interesting experiences for the Bernys. Both recalled a Mrs. McCann who

ABOVE: Catching up on the news from home were Mr. and Mrs. F. M. Wilmot of Pittsburgh, Pennsylvania. Wilmot was manager, secretary, and commissioner of the Carnegie Hero Fund Commission. He and his wife were spending several months at The Vinoy Park Hotel in the late 1930s.

LEFT: Guests enjoyed the Vinoy's swimming pool, lounging poolside, and chatting with friends. Then, as now, pool attendants came by to spritz them with cool water. However, more serious sun worshippers paid about thirty-five cents to use the hotel's solariums for nude sunbathing. The solariums (the one in the photo is located on the right above the pool) were on wheels so that hotel staff could turn them to catch the sun's rays as it moved across the sky. Registered nurses were in attendance because sunbathing was often prescribed as a medical cure for arthritis, neuritis, sinus trouble, rheumatism, and respiratory diseases. Each booth was equipped with a chair, a cot, and a towel. The towels could be used for a "quick cover up" when planes flew overhead. Occasionally children at the hotel were caught on the roof peering down into the solariums with telescopes.

Photo from the Renaissance Vinoy Resort Archives

owned Canada Dry and Domino Sugar Company. She was an extremely generous woman, tipping the elevator operators $5 which was a significant amount of money in the 1930s. Her chauffeur, Arthur, was Michael Berny's friend. After the crash, Arthur revealed that Mrs. McCann didn't have any cash because of the bank closures. Without hesitation, Michael Berny gave her all the cash he had, $30 to $50. She later repaid him by purchasing $3,000 worth of merchandise from his shop, an incredible transaction since, according to the Bernys, his sales for the entire season usually totaled $5,000.

Steve Berny shared another story of a wealthy woman from Chicago who bought a $165 tablecloth on approval. The next season she wanted to return it. Michael Berny didn't want the cloth back and she didn't want to pay for it. Instead of paying cash for the tablecloth, she offered Berny 160 acres of land she owned in Fort Myers. He agreed.

The staff closed the hotel following its fifteenth season in April of 1941. Rumblings of the war in Europe were growing louder, but no one here was concerned. The Vinoy Park Hotel had sailed through the economic recession of 1926 and the Great Depression. Reservations were steady. The future looked bright. The Florida sun was shining and surely everything was fine.

Or was it?

RIGHT: By the 1930s, The Vinoy Park Hotel was an integral part of St. Petersburg's social scene and photographed often not only as the site of newsworthy parties and balls, but even as the backdrop for fashion shows and "shoots." This photo titled "Three Babes at the Vinoy" was hand-painted by artist Lorraine Genovar.

OPPOSITE
TOP: Shortly after the Vinoy reopened in 1992, a former bellman (third man from the left) donated this photograph of the uniformed staff taken in the 1930s. The jackets, made of 100 percent wool, were not only heavy, but durable and warm. Hotel lore has it that on especially cold days, one of the bellmen would hurry to the loggia, strike a match and hold it to the thermometer elevating the temperature so guests would think the weather warmer than it actually was.

BOTTOM: St. Petersburg's waterfront, still dominated by The Vinoy Park, dozed in the sun in this aerial photo taken in 1940. Soon the clouds of war would transform the city, the people, and the hotel.

44

Photo courtesy of Lorraine Genovar

Photo from the Renaissance Vinoy Resort Archives

Photo from the Renaissance Vinoy Resort Archives

THE MEAN SEASONS

RONICALLY, THE VINOY PARK HOTEL had sailed through the crippling depression years. The economic crisis that had brought our young, strong nation to its knees had little effect on the wealthy families who still arrived every December to winter at the Vinoy. It took World War II, a battle fought on foreign lands and seas, to threaten to sink the Vinoy.

In a letter to the stockholders of The Vinoy Park Hotel Company dated May 12, 1942, A. V. Laughner wrote, "On April 1, 1942, Vinoy Park Hotel completed its seventeenth season of operation. Business during the season was the poorest of any year since 1927." He was not over reacting.

Laughner went on to explain that the business decline was due almost entirely to World War II. "Prior to December 7, 1941, our reservations were good and we confidently expected that we would again enjoy a business equal at least to that of 1941," he wrote. The operating profit for the 1942 season was $14,000 compared to $111,450 for the 1941 season. Gross business was approximately fifty-five percent of the previous season and the number of guests had dropped by approximately fifty percent.

The impact was devastating. Not only was the operating profit insufficient to meet basic operating expenses, it failed to cover the cost of summer maintenance which totaled $16,650 as well as an expenditure of $1,050 for new equipment not to mention real estate taxes, federal income tax, payroll taxes, and interest on the $90,000 mortgage held by Charles T. and Harold S. Clark of the Clark Candy Company of Pittsburgh, Pennsylvania. As a result of this shortfall, Laughner reported he'd made arrangements to refinance the hotel's debt with the Union Trust Company of St. Petersburg at an interest rate not to exceed four percent per annum.

Another blow was the departure of Clement Kennedy who had served as manager for fourteen years prior to being called for duty in the U.S. Army on September 10, 1941. Laughner stepped in personally to fulfill Kennedy's duties and operate the hotel.

PREVIOUS SPREAD: While it was business as usual following the end of World War II, change—inexorable and irrevocable—was on the way.

OPPOSITE: As the 1941 season opened, dark war clouds swirled around the United States and would soon have a devastating impact on The Vinoy Park Hotel.

As bleak as the situation appeared, help in the personage of Uncle Sam was on the way. In the spring of 1941, Pinellas County had begun construction of an airport on a 939-acre tract of county-owned land on the west shore of Tampa Bay. After Pearl Harbor, the airport was named the Pinellas Army Air Field and designated the home base for combat training for the 304th and 440th Fighter Squadrons.

The airspace over Pinellas County was soon crowded with P-40s and later P-51s. The pervasiveness of the nation's military presence in Florida, let alone Pinellas County, could not be overestimated. In 1940, Florida had contained eight military bases. By 1943, that number had swollen to an incredible 172. The streets of towns and cities across the state—St. Petersburg among them—were crammed and jammed and bustling with khaki-uniformed servicemen. The men had to stay somewhere and the answer to that problem proved to be

RIGHT: When the hotels overflowed, a tent city was established on the grounds of The Vinoy Park.

OPPOSITE: Hup, two, three, four. Hour after hour, the troops drilled along the bayfront passing the entrance to the Vinoy where many were stationed. They were a strange contrast to the chauffeur-driven Packards and Daimlers and Rolls Royces that had traveled these same streets in peace time.

Photo courtesy of St. Petersburg Historical Museum

the solution for many of Florida's beleaguered resort hotels including The Vinoy Park.

Desperate to find housing for its men, the U.S. Army Air Corps established The Vinoy Park as its local headquarters and leased every hotel of any size including many of the smaller hostelries, except for the Suwannee. Even then when the military population swelled to more than ten thousand, a "tent city" was erected on the grounds of the Vinoy to house the overflow.

In his annual report to the stockholders on May 11, 1943, Laughner wrote, "The Vinoy Park Hotel did not operate as a resort hotel during the past winter. The property of the corporation was leased to the U.S. War Department on July 3, 1942, and since that time has been used as quarters for soldiers of the Army Air Forces Technical Training Center which has been established in St. Petersburg."

Laughner's ambivalence and concern were obvious as he continued, "This lease was made against the better judgment of the officers and directors of the company, and was done mainly as a contribution to the war effort." He wrote of "hard wear" from the soldiers adding that a large part of the furniture would be so damaged it would not be usable. However, the news wasn't all bad—the hotel's indebtedness in one year had been reduced from $153,708.83 to $96,881.01.

The "hard wear" Laughner mentioned was not an exaggeration. Norman Weyer, for many years after World War II a baking instructor at the Pinellas Technical Education Center at the St. Petersburg Campus, was stationed at the Vinoy as one of two baking instructors assigned to teach a two-month course to Air Force personnel. While the hotel had left the furniture, Weyer recalls, "The hotel had removed all rugs and floor coverings before they leased the hotel to the Air Force and, as was the custom in that time, we had to 'GI' the floors every day—soap and water and elbow grease." This practice played havoc with the finish on the maple floors in the ballroom. The lovely murals were painted over. Young, restless soldiers lying on their bunk beds kicked holes in the plaster. The thunder of thousands of footfalls reverberated through the previously peaceful corridors shaking the staid hotel to its foundation.

Civilians were involved in the Vinoy's war efforts as well. Longtime St. Petersburg resident Bobbi O'Malley remembers that she and her grandmother Allie Newman did their civic duty serving as plane spotters stationed on the Vinoy's roof while her grandfather, Mac Newman, served as an air raid warden.

In the huge ovens below, Weyer's trainees learned to bake bread, rolls, cinnamon buns, and pies. Pastries were baked in the kitchen, but the ovens were located in what is now the laundry. One of his most indelible memories is of the servicemen marching at Straub Park in front of the Vinoy. As they marched, they sang, filling the air with the strains of the Air Force anthem, "Off We Go Into The Wild Blue Yonder."

Weyer's memories also include a group of very special young women sponsored by the USO and dubbed "The Bomb-a-Dears." Composed of local young ladies, the rigidly chaperoned group was transported by Army truck to dances at various bases including the Vinoy where they served as dancing partners for the soldiers. Ellen J. Babb writing about St. Petersburg women during World War II for THE FLORIDA HISTORICAL QUARTERLY, said of the Bomb-a-Dears that it was the largest of three junior affiliates of the Defense

Photo courtesy of Norman Weyer

Norman Weyer, baking instructor, was stationed at the Vinoy during World War II.

Mothers organization with more than four hundred members in 1943. "The club had its own weekly column in the St. Petersburg Times and held dances, dinner parties, and other forms of entertainment for the soldiers. Before they were eligible to volunteer with this service organization, young women were required to present references attesting to their moral character. Most of the new recruits came from local high schools and the junior college."

Weyer has a special fondness for the Bomb-a-Dears since his wife was one of those patriotic lasses. After his tour of duty at the Vinoy, Weyer was reassigned to Fort Benning, Georgia. After the war, Weyer, a native of Ferdnand, Indiana, returned to St. Petersburg.

Another former GI with indelible memories of the Vinoy is Kenneth E. Walden of McLean, Virginia. The hotel had been occupied by the U.S. Army Air Corps until August 1, 1943, when the lease was transferred to the War Shipping Administration. The WSA, in turn, assigned use of the Vinoy to the U.S. Maritime Training Service.

Photo courtesy of Mrs. Sam Mann

Mr. and Mrs. Wally Bishop of nearby Snell Isle rode their bicycle built for two to visit friends staying in the Vinoy in 1937. Mr. Bishop was a well known cartoonist famous for his comic strip "Mugs & Skeeter." The character Skeeter was based on the couple's daughter Mary Joan Mann who recently loaned this photo to the Vinoy during their 75th anniversary memorabilia search.

Walden arrived by train from Kansas City on October 21, 1943, along with about thirty other Maritime recruits. Life was to be drastically different for these "guests."

"We were met in St. Petersburg's train station by a Maritime Service open-bedded trailer truck. I have no recall of what happened for the remainder of the day, but I do recall the next day fairly vividly.

"We were processed: stripped, poked, examined, shots, hair cuts. New clothes (some fit, some didn't) were thrown at us in a limited effort at approximately the right sizes. Our group was mixed with possibly two other groups to form a unit with a number something like 258. We had a permanent crew leader who was with us all the time. As far as we were concerned, he was the only person we could look to for everything. I've long ago forgotten his name, but he was a-okay. He marched us to whatever classes we were attending. We marched everywhere; we were never allowed to wander.

"The hotel was beautiful from the outside," he writes, adding, "but the inside had been gutted, and I mean gutted, to remove anything of the appearance of luxury." There were no chairs in the lobby or the rooms. "I have only a glint of recall of ever being in the lobby for I'm not sure trainees were permitted there." Photos for identification and passports were taken on the mezzanine and he does recall being able to sit in a chair for those sittings.

As for the elevators today's guests take for granted, while they certainly existed and functioned properly, Walden doesn't remember using them, but poses the rhetorical question, "What 19-year-old boy wants an elevator when he can make better time up or down via the stairs?" However, he adds that in a recent conversation with a

Kenneth E. Walden, stationed at the Vinoy during World War II, shared his Identification Card as issued by the Captain of the Port of St. Petersburg.

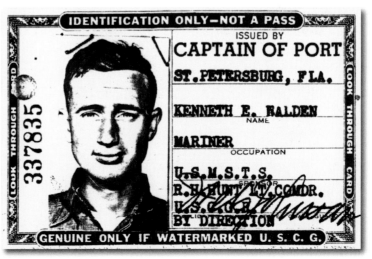

Photo courtesy of Kenneth E. Walden

serviceman from the unit that followed his, he was told only Maritime officers could use the elevators.

Five trainees were assigned to each room and while he remembers there was nothing like a chest of drawers, he says, "Most likely there were Army-like bunks in the room … About all I recall from that room is sitting on my cot and listening to the 'big boys' talk about girls. They knew all about them! I tried to keep my mouth shut so as not to expose my innocent past."

The bathroom had a tub which all five used. "Life was not intentionally made nice for us and that was brought out by inspections necessary for weekend passes. Any infraction regarding cleanliness in a room automatically meant no pass. We had from somewhere cleaning equipment and materials for the rooms, but what was one to do with a cleaning cloth that was used to clean the bathtub? Hide it somewhere? No way. There was no such thing as a waste basket. So therein was a constant problem because the permanent crew examined every nook and crevice. One weekend our room was 'gigged' and denied a liberty because of a single hair that was noted in the tub."

Classes were held in the open air on plank seating supported above the sand. "The instruction," Walden writes, "was just basic stuff since cargo ships don't carry 16-inch guns. Some First Aid, swimming, marching."

After two months at the Vinoy and two weeks on an "old, old ship named 'The Seafarer,'" Walden shipped out. He was, however, accepted in the Army Transport Cadet School and ultimately assigned as an engineering officer on a small cargo ship.

On the menu for Thanksgiving and Christmas in 1943 were all-American favorites: turkey and sage dressing, giblet gravy, cranberry sauce, candied sweet potatoes, mince pie, and pumpkin pie.

Courtesy of Kenneth Walden

On March 1, 1944, Laughner was informed the government intended to cancel its lease as of April 1, 1944. He included this datum in his annual letter to the stockholders that May adding, "The cancellation has not been revoked, but we do not yet have possession." The government, he explained, was required by the terms of the lease to complete certain restoration and repair of damages before returning the hotel to the company's possession. The restoration and repair had been started and, although it was progressing slowly, the fifth and sixth floors were nearly finished and the work was satisfactory.

He further reported he had been approached by "representatives of the U.S. Maritime Service to consider a cash settlement of damages rather than requiring the government to complete the work …" A contractor had estimated the amount of damage and the company was now ready to negotiate.

The good news was twofold: Laughner was planning to open for business as usual in December 1944, and the mortgage had been paid

Photo from the Renaissance Vinoy Resort Archives

in full. Sterling Bottome stepped in as manager and it looked as though everything would continue as before. The war, however, was winding down and change was on the horizon—not only for the Vinoy, but for the entire hospitality industry.

In an interview published in the July 30, 1992, edition of the St. Petersburg Times, Laughner's son Paul told a reporter, "My father was getting older and tired of it. He was never a hotel man."

Aymer Vinoy Laughner had earned a rest. Despite not being a hotel man, he had not only "birthed" the splendid hotel, he had shepherded it through the treacherous shoals of its early years of financial ups and downs as well as the difficult war years. And now the hotel had a suitor. Charles H. Alberding, a businessman from Chicago, had been enamored of the Vinoy for several years. In fact, he had tried to buy the Vinoy even before it was on the market. At that time, local real estate agent Charles Crisp convinced him to buy The Tides Hotel and Bath Club Resort on the beach. Now, with Laughner ready and anxious to step down, Alberding stepped up.

OPPOSITE: The grand ballroom had been restored and the maple floor had been refinished. No trace of the military presence remained.

LEFT: The brilliant colors of ancient Pompeii had been restored in the dining room, the china had been brought out of storage along with the fixtures. New carpet had been laid and looking at this elegant room, it was hard to believe it had ever been occupied by the Army Air Corps. Just as the builder had worked with speed and dispatch to complete the hotel ahead of schedule in 1925, twenty years later, Vinoy and Bottome and their staff worked frantically during the summer and fall of 1944 in order to open on time and in good order for the 1944–1945 season.

OVERLEAF: The grand ballroom was once again the scene of dances where the men wore dinner jackets instead of khaki uniforms and their dates weren't brought in by Army transport.

57

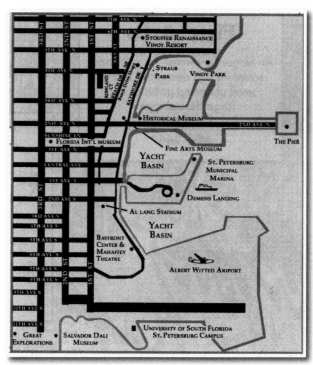

Map from Renaissance Vinoy Resort files

ABOVE: Map showing the location of the Vinoy.

RIGHT: The occasion was baseball great Connie Mack's (left) eighty-third birthday in 1945 which was marked with a gala dinner at the Vinoy attended by Mack's longtime friend Al F. Lang (right). Lang, who moved to St. Petersburg in 1910, worked tirelessly and successfully to bring major league teams to St. Petersburg for spring training. Al Lang Field is named to honor him.

OPPOSITE: This postcard mailed in February 1945 depicts St. Petersburg's Recreation Pier which extended a half-mile into Tampa Bay. The casino is in the foreground, the Vinoy in the background. The message on the back revealed that for some guests, little had changed. It read, "Dear Ruth, I have no news this morning. Am going to a party this p.m. It is right here in the hotel. Will write you later all about it. It is only two tables of bridge."

Photo from Renaissance Vinoy Resort Archives

Recreation Pier, St. Petersburg, Fla.

Photo from the Renaissance Vinoy Resort Archives

Alberding had been born March 5, 1901, in Clayville, New York. One of seven children, he attended Cornell University where he played varsity soccer, basketball, and hockey. After graduating from Cornell in 1923 with a degree in electrical engineering, he accepted a position in the oil industry. By 1928, he'd become so knowledgeable he'd been offered a job with Universal Oil Products. The company sent him to head up their London office where his job was to design and start up oil refineries. He had done this all around the world— Italy, Romania, Burma—traveling constantly.

"Because of his extensive traveling, his love of the Latin and Greek classics and the European architecture and the different hotels … I think at some point in the late 1930s, he decided he'd been with Universal Oil long enough and he wanted to break away," his daughter Melissa Moore explained. "His idea was to get into the hotel and travel industry.

"With that goal in mind, in the early 1940s he put together a group of advisors and managers and began picking up and running commercial hotels in the areas he'd traveled while in the oil business—Texas, Oklahoma, Colorado, Wyoming, and Michigan. In the early years, he owned about forty-nine hotels at one time although the number would fluctuate as he bought and sold.

Charles H. Alberding, who bought The Vinoy Park Hotel in 1945, was an astute if controversial businessman known as a tough negotiator whose talents spanned several industries. He began his business career in elementary school with a paper route, but soon convinced his father to give him space in the family farm equipment store so he could sell baseball gloves. He later worked in a textile mill and paid his living expenses at Cornell by washing dishes, waiting on tables, and looking after a professor's furnace. During World War II, he served on the War Production Board and as petroleum administrator for sixteen states from 1943–1945.

After a successful twenty-five-year career in the oil business, he and partner D. L. Connett formed the Alsonett Hotel chain and at one time owned forty-nine different hotels all over the country. An athlete who played semi-pro baseball until he was twenty-five, he was named to the Cornell University Athletic Hall of Fame and, along with former Senator Barry Goldwater, he initiated the application for the Fiesta Bowl in Phoenix, Arizona. He organized a National Association of Intercollegiate Athletics football bowl game called the Holiday Bowl which was held for two years in St. Petersburg. On May 2, 1920, he married Bethine Wolverton. Mr. and Mrs. Alberding had three daughters; Beth Ann Mohr-Hansen, Mary R. Cartwright, and Melissa Moore.

Photo courtesy of Melissa Moore

"I think it was about 1942 when he came to Florida and started looking around," Melissa Moore remembers. "The Vinoy was the kind of hotel he just loved. He ended up with six or seven resort hotels, but the Vinoy was a nice addition and not only was he proud of the Vinoy, he loved the Vinoy."

The purchase price was $700,000 and the deal was sealed in September 1945. Outwardly everything continued as before. Bottome stayed on as manager so the service was meticulous and the food was superb as was the music. The time once again was gentle and innocent. The Vinoy fill was no longer crowded with row upon row of khaki-clad marching soldiers. Now it was a favorite place for St. Petersburg teenagers to park and watch the "submarine races." Mary Joan Mann remembers that one of the local boys had a black Chevrolet with a spotlight mounted on the front. He would flash the light into the front seats of the lovers' cars making them think they'd been apprehended by the long arm of the law.

The winter guests returned year after year and local residents embraced the Vinoy as the backdrop for the special moments of their lives—wedding receptions, banquets, debutante balls, and New Year's Eve parties.

Weddings and baked delicacies continued as a Vinoy tradition.

TOP: Proud parents waited with their well-dressed offspring in front of the Vinoy as these children waited for the signal to move into parade formation during the Festival of States parade.

BOTTOM: The Queen of Hearts, a charming St. Petersburg lass, was ready for the Festival of States parade which started in front of the Vinoy.

OPPOSITE: An important part of the hotel business is traveling to trade shows to publicize your properties. According to Mrs. Moore, this traveling display which highlighted his Florida hotels including The Vinoy Park was very effective and was taken to industry shows all around the country.

Photo courtesy of Melissa Moore

TOP: From debutantes to the Dragon Club to The Quarterback Club, The Vinoy Park was the scene of a variety of social events involving many different segments of St. Petersburg society.

BOTTOM: This photograph was taken from The Vinoy Park mezzanine in February 1949. St. Petersburg was rebounding from World War II which had ended a scant four years earlier. Building permits for homes and apartment buildings were growing annually now that building supplies were available, the trolleys had been "retired," the new Maas Brothers Department Store had opened, and the Federal Census of 1950 would reveal that during the previous decade the population had grown from 60,812 to 96,838, but it was business as usual at the Vinoy.

OPPOSITE

TOP: A quiet moment in the Vinoy cocktail lounge gave the master mixologist an opportunity to get organized for the evening. The colorful mural on the wall set the nautical theme.

BOTTOM: The Vinoy Park Hotel was featured prominently in this postcard listing Alsonett properties and dating back to the 1950s.

Photo courtesy of Melissa Moore

Courtesy of Melissa Moore

Thirty years after its opening, the rates seemed far more reasonable. When the hotel reopened on December 8, 1954 for its twenty-ninth season, the weekly rates ranged from $112 for single occupancy of a double room to a high of $154. The rate for double rooms with twin beds ranged from $154 to $224. The rates were under the American Plan which included meals. Daily rates were one-seventh of the weekly rate plus $2 per day per person. An additional $1 per person per day was charged for corner rooms. Amenities included motor boating, sailing, yachting, fishing, horseback riding, putting, dancing, shuffleboard, concert music, bridge, "Vinoy" (a form of Bingo), greyhound racing, sun bathing and golf at three 18-hole courses including the Sunset Golf Club. According to Melissa Moore, the rates reflected her father's desire to make luxury and beauty accessible to more people of average means.

BOTTOM: The lawn was an excellent place to practice one's putting.

Opposite
TOP: Lovely girls in bathing suits wearing pretty smiles were good business advertisements in the 1950s.

BOTTOM: The shuffleboard courts were a popular attraction.

Photo from the Renaissance Vinoy Resort Archives

Photo from the Renaissance Vinoy Resort Archives

The quest for excellence remained constant. In a letter to Bottome dated November 1, 1965, Harry van Haam, the Vinoy's musical director, wrote, "I am more than pleased to be able to tell you that the music is all set for the coming season at the Vinoy. It was not easy to locate a fine 'cellist, but it was done ... I have just returned from two weeks in New York and Boston, the above work being my principal occupation." Van Haam went on to say the man he had hired was "presently playing at the Colonial Theatre, the best Boston engagement outside the Boston Symphony ... He does not play bass for the dances however, so I have offered him less pay, so you will save $10 weekly."

On December 20, 1968, Bottome relinquished the managerial reins to David L. Johnson, but remained on hand as vice president and a director of The Vinoy Park Hotel Company representing the stockholders. As with Laughner decades earlier, it was a well-earned

By 1955, the lobby had been refurbished. The original fixtures remained, but the furniture and the carpeting had been replaced and the palms and foliage were added.

respite for Bottome had been with Aymer Vinoy Laughner and involved with the hotel as far back as its planning and construction stages in 1925.

Johnson was no stranger to the Vinoy either. He'd been Bottome's assistant since 1949 and had started in the hotel business at the age of fourteen in a New Hampshire hotel. The 1968–1969 season opened as usual with a modicum of fanfare and the illumination of the red light in the Vinoy's tower. "Starting crews were at their posts yesterday at 8 a.m. or earlier, and another winter season was under way," wrote columnist Paul Davis in the ST. PETERSBURG INDEPENDENT.

Johnson told Davis the hotel's interior had been refurbished during the summer. Equipment had been replaced where needed and the hotel was in tiptop shape. Johnson said he anticipated a good season and added the season's closing date would be April 7.

Photo from the Renaissance Vinoy Resort Archives

Photo from the Renaissance Vinoy archives

But time and change, however gradual, were marching forward as inexorably as had the platoons of soldiers two decades earlier. The country was experiencing a wave of unprecedented prosperity that encompassed the middle class and America was on the move. People who previously couldn't afford vacations were now hitting the country's burgeoning superhighways in their automobiles. But they weren't staying in luxury resorts like the Vinoy. Instead they registered by the tens of thousands in the highway motels where you carried your own luggage, got your own ice, where you stayed only one or two nights, and moved on. These guests did not dress for dinner, order corsages to wear each evening, or keep their good jewelry in the hotel vault.

Then too, the socialites whose storied names had graced the Vinoy's guest registers since its opening were dying and their children no longer wanted to spend the winter in one resort. The youngsters were taking shorter trips and more of them. Air transportation had become so convenient and comfortable that they could fly to Paris for the weekend, to Rio for the carnival, to Monte Carlo for a weekend of gambling, or escape to Gstaad for a few days on the ski slopes.

OPPOSITE: The loggia was still the place for a pleasant afternoon chat, but the guests were growing older and many were the widows of the famous men who'd once wintered at the hotel.

LEFT: One sign of change was the Life of Georgia Convention held at the Vinoy in April 1951. Delegates numbering 330 and their wives were photographed on the front lawn as Life of Georgia marked its sixtieth anniversary with a gala weekend. The arrival of these conventioneers was an indication that the hotel business was changing, that it might be necessary to court conventions to make up for the loss by attrition of the guests who spent the entire season.

OVERLEAF
LEFT: By the 1950s, a green canvas canopy had been added to shield guests from inclement weather, but perhaps the biggest change was the fact that family sedans were now more prevalent than the chauffeured limousines of past years.

RIGHT: Although the Guggenheim yacht no longer spent the season in the Vinoy's marina, smaller pleasure boats rocked at anchor in the placid, sheltered waters of Tampa Bay.

Photo from the Renaissance Vinoy Resort Archives

As a result, the Vinoy and its fortunes were slowly declining. The problems weren't just the result of the shorter stays and the variety of vacation destinations its former mainstay guests were choosing. The hotel itself was outdated. The fifteen-by-fourteen-foot rooms had never been considered spacious and now they were too small to compete with other hotels and motels. The lack of air conditioning created still another problem.

The community complained that Alberding was not maintaining the hotel, that he was an absentee landlord. Alberding, a very private man, refused to explain but Melissa Moore says, "After the 1960s, I think my father realized the hotel was always closed in the summer and the season was getting shorter and the reservations weren't coming in … he loved the hotel and didn't want to sell, but he was putting every penny he made there back into the hotel and at that point he had to think of the alternatives. It was hard for him to let go, but he had other businesses."

By now it was early 1972 and a new player entered the scene. Bob Reynolds had grown up with the Vinoy. Like Alberding, he'd fallen in love with the hotel, but he was only twenty.

"When I was only five years old," Reynolds said, "I told somebody the hotel reminded me of a big castle and I told my Dad I wanted to own the Vinoy. He said 'That's good, son.'

"By the 1970s, condos were taking off and I saw the Vinoy's par 3 golf course as a tremendous site for condos. Harry Waldron, owner of Shaeffer Pen Company was a close friend of the family. I talked to him about it and he said, 'Well, go talk to C. H. Alberding and see if he won't sell it to you.'"

The handmade tile floor was inlaid with smaller pieces which recall French heraldry.

"I took $10,000 in cash and went to Mr. Alberding and said, 'I want to buy the Vinoy.' To my surprise, he said, 'Yes.'" The deal was a six-month option to purchase the hotel for $5 million.

Of course, as Reynolds explains, there was more to it than that. "I had originally gone to Dad and he said, 'Are you nuts?' I said again, 'Dad, I'm going to buy the Vinoy.' Within an hour and a half, he had talked to four of his friends and he came into the deal with me."

The group formed R. W. Enterprises, Inc. with a board composed of his father, C. J. Reynolds, J. Rogers Badgett of Badgett Coal Mines in Evansville, Indiana, Lee F. Powell and Harold Woodall of Paducah, Kentucky.

Reynolds found Alberding extremely easy and pleasant to work with and the two men became friends, but the deal itself launched Reynolds into eight years of financial and emotional upheaval.

As his next step, he went to local architect C. Randolph Wedding to draw up plans for the hotel. Wedding even invited the young entrepreneur to use his office and ultimately became deeply involved in the project to the point where he was treasurer. Wedding drew plans for the hotel's renovation as well as three condominium towers and also ran—successfully—for mayor of St. Petersburg, a fact which would hinder rather than enhance his effectiveness because of the constant potential for conflict of interest.

Reynolds obtained a $5 million commitment from Ford Motor Company, but had to turn it down. "My board didn't feel it was pru-

The Vinoy Park Hotel was often the scene for St. Petersburg's debutante balls, a longtime tradition. One of the loveliest was this Debutantes Ball held in 1970. The theme was roses and the debutantes in the front row were (left to right): Rebecca Stone Bishop escorted by Harold Elliot Barrett; Eleanor Frances Bussey escorted by William Kimberly Bennett; Barbara Lynn Hobach escorted by Richard Ryan Bowers; Pamela Newton Howe escorted by Henry Shaughan Stokes; Mary Elizabeth Mann escorted by James Lee West III; Catherine Jane Pilkington escorted by Jeffrey Gerald Wolfe; and Marcia Bassett Yon escorted by Paul Douglas Maglian.

dent to accept the Ford commitment to purchase the hotel without having a commitment for financing to renovate the hotel or build the condos," he says.

He obtained a commitment to build the condos, but since part of that deal involved razing the hotel, he turned it down incurring the wrath of his board. He went back to his friend Alberding who suggested that if they didn't want to take the Ford commitment to outright purchase the property, they might consider a ninety-nine-year lease. They worked a deal based on eight and three-quarters percent interest and $437,5000 a year.

According to Reynolds, a rift developed among board members, some of whom were not as dedicated to saving the Vinoy as he and his father. Then, too, progress was slow and finally in 1974, they closed the Vinoy, ostensibly for renovation. For the first time during peacetime, the grand hotel was silent and dark.

Not long after that, they took in Joseph Campagna, a St. Louis developer who promised to secure financing for the $40 million complex they were planning.

In December of 1975, Reynolds, advised by Wedding and Campagna, reopened the once proud hotel, slashing the rates from $50 a night the previous year to $7 a night to help pay for the proposed facelift. The chairs and tables and the piano in the grand ball-

When published on July 1, 1975, this photo of a volleyball game being played in the grand ballroom belied the optimism of the caption which read, "The splendor of the past may soon be recaptured in downtown St. Petersburg. Developers said yesterday they are completing a deal for funds to restore the Vinoy Park Hotel to its former status as a showcase resort. In the meantime, innovative athletes are using its immense ballroom as a volleyball court."

78

Photo courtesy of the St. Petersburg Times

room were pushed aside. The beautiful rug with its floral pattern had been slashed to reveal the maple floor and a net had been strung. The ballroom, once the site of debutante balls and glamorous social events, was now used for public dances and card parties and even as a volleyball court. The corridors that had once echoed with the footsteps of our nation's wealthiest and most renowned citizens were now deserted and forlorn; empty except for Tuesday and Thursday nights when the volleyball games were played to bring in bar business.

The St. Petersburg Times reported that open houses held during two weekends had drawn about four thousand people and Joseph A. Campagna, now president of R. W. Enterprises, Inc., said the hotel might soon be sold out for the winter season. That turned out to be wishful thinking because it closed in 1975 and the following year, St. Petersburg Times Staff Writer Timothy M. Phelps wrote these sad words, "Tea will not be served at 4 at the Vinoy this winter. It will not be served at all … the Cadillacs will not grace the drive. The gentlemen will not exercise on the putting greens or the croquet lawn. And the ladies will miss high tea at 4."

But the bills kept piling up and finally Campagna, with Wedding's support against Reynolds, auctioned off all the hotel's furniture, equipment, and anything that wasn't part of the structure. As 1975 ended, the fiftieth anniversary of the grand hotel was a sad shadow of its glittering opening.

But Reynolds and his group struggled on. In September 1978, The Vinoy Park Hotel was named to the National Register of Historic Places and Wedding held press conferences in which he emphasized the possibility of finding financiers who could now take advantage of the tax breaks inherent in restoring an historic property. But the hotel and R. W. Enterprises, Inc. were in serious trouble. Back taxes were due, Barnett Bank was foreclosing, and Alberding had sued because of the sale of the hotel's furniture and equipment.

By 1980, the Vinoy's guests were vagrants and derelicts. SWAT teams from local police departments utilized the upper floors to rehearse shoot-and-enter training scenarios. Instead of a security staff, the hotel was protected by guard dogs and fences, but another developer was on the horizon and by this time Alberding had run out of patience.

Alberding cancelled the lease and Reynolds' boyhood dream of owning The Vinoy Park Hotel, a dream that had taken eight years of his life, was finally over. "I tried awfully hard," he said.

OVERLEAF: The Vinoy would be closed for seventeen years. During that time, weeds overpowered the exotic plants and tropical shrubs once so carefully planted and maintained. By 1978, when this photo was taken, the beautiful hotel was an eyesore.

SAVE THE VINOY

HE VINOY'S FUTURE WAS FAR FROM secure as the decade of the 1980s began and the story of the hotel's renovation and reopening would prove to be a tangled, winding plot laced with so many complications, false starts, misdeeds, financial disasters, and pitfalls that it reads more like a fascinating, suspense novel.

After deciding not to renew the lease with R. W. Reynolds Enterprises, Alberding had leased the Vinoy to Gulfport developer Arthur H. Padula and St. Petersburg businessman Robert V. Workman. The plan once again was to restore and operate The Vinoy Park Hotel and, this time, to build five hundred condominiums in two sixteen-story buildings on land east of the resort.

By June 1981 and after months and months of proposals and counter proposals, the St. Petersburg City Council approved Padula's

PREVIOUS SPREAD: The Vinoy's once elegant lobby and promenade would be restored to her former glory as the determined efforts of developers began to succeed.

By the late 1970s, the dormitory, the three-story building on the far right, had been condemned by the city of St. Petersburg. Built in 1925–1926 to house the Vinoy's staff, the dormitory was demolished on September 18, 1980, because the foundation was crumbling and it had become a sanctuary for derelicts and vandals.

84

plan, but that was just the first step in a long, involved process. The land would have to be rezoned, the site plan would have to be approved by the Environmental Development Commission and public hearings would have to be held, but the city council had at last made a decision and Padula was elated. His elation was to be short-lived, however, for within the month the city would kill the project. This time it was not the city's stance on growth, but the receipt of a letter apparently sent by one of Padula's investors.

The letter, a Telex, was supposedly a letter of commitment to restore and manage the Vinoy from an international corporation that operated hotels. When the St. Petersburg City Manager contacted the corporation, to his surprise, he was informed they had neither authored not authorized the letter. While the explanation was proffered that it was transmitted by error and that the Telex was not intended as "misrepresentation or misleading," the city council's confidence in Padula was shattered.

Next Alberding took matters into his own hands and, instead of waiting for prospects to come to him he contacted Craig McLaughlin, then president of B. B. Andersen Development Company headquartered in Kansas. B. B. Andersen had done the historic renovation on three of Alberding's other properties—The Hermitage in Nashville, Tennessee; the Charleston Hotel in Lake Charles, Louisiana; and The JayHawk in Topeka, Kansas. As a result, he was familiar with the company and its executives.

"We had an option and we examined the property, ran the numbers and decided we were too far ahead of the market—five or six years," McLaughlin said in an interview conducted while this book was being researched. "We did not exercise the option and Alberding leased to another person who had been waiting to move forward—J. J. Palumbo."

Palumbo, a Cincinnati-based businessman, hired B. B. Andersen in May of 1982 to repair the roof and to clean and board up the hotel so that it would be secure and avoid further damage. This was a very necessary step because the city council was continuing to threaten condemnation.

Just as things seemed to be going well for the beleaguered hotel, Federal regulators stepped in and took over Palumbo's Sparta-Sanders Bank in Kentucky temporarily crippling him financially. At that point, B. B. Andersen started working with the State Savings and Loan Company of Lubbock, Texas. Andersen signed a lease with Alberding and within an hour of signing and making a deposit on that lease, Alberding received a call from Harold Geneen.

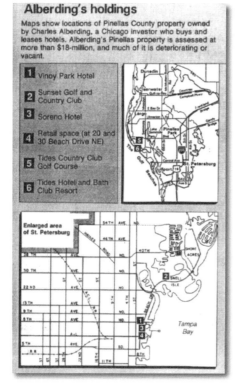

Courtesy of Melissa Moore and the ST. PETERSBURG TIMES

ABOVE: A list of Alberding's holdings.

RIGHT: The Vinoy's sad state of deterioration prior to restoration was vividly displayed in this photo.

Geneen, recently retired as president and chief executive officer of International Telephone and Telegraph, had joined forces with Fred Guest and Bert Stephens in an earlier attempt to buy the Boca Raton Hotel on Florida's East Coast. They had been too late by about a week. When Stephens, who had worked with Alberding in the 1950s, learned of the Vinoy's plight and availability, he contacted Guest. "The only problem," Guest said in an interview published in the September 1990 issue of TAMPA BAY LIFE magazine, "(is that) it was in trouble and closed."

Guest was a man of impeccable background and connections, a retired stockbroker, investor, and investment banker. A 1960 graduate of the Wharton School of Business, he was also a relative of Winston Churchill. His great grandfather was Andrew Carnegie's partner and his mother was F. W. Woolworth's granddaughter. After his first retirement, he had helped start the New York State Urban Development Corporation to speed up low-cost housing construction and town redevelopment. He left that position to help his family's company, Bessemer Securities Corporation, which was experiencing problems with a land company.

After resolving those problems, Guest went on to help establish Bessemer Trust Company. Since providing banking and investment services just for the family had proved to be very expensive, Guest and the Bessemer Trust applied for and received a charter as a new bank in New York. The Bessemer Trust became extremely successful with minimum accounts of $5 million and Guest had again retired.

Now, despite the drawbacks, Guest traveled to St. Petersburg with Geneen to look at the Vinoy. "I immediately fell in love with it," he said in the article. "Mr. Geneen wished me good luck, but said he didn't do development deals." Guest and Stephens decided to move forward with Andersen.

"At this point, B. B. Andersen closed on a construction loan with State Savings and Loan and formed The Vinoy Park Partnership," McLaughlin said. "We spent about $6 million on lease acquisition, repairing roofs, putting in windows and getting the interior in condition so we could start to rebuild. We hired the architect—the whole shooting match."

As with Palumbo, the uncertain economy of the 1980s threw not merely a monkey wrench but an entire toolkit into the works. "The bank got into trouble," McLaughlin said, "and after drawing $6 million of the $36 to $46 million construction loan, the bank was insolvent." Because of the bank's insolvency, all work stopped.

In addition, McLaughlin had decided to go into business for himself so he left Andersen to form his own company. Once McLaughin was out of the picture, differences arose between Guest and Stephens and Andersen with the result that the parties agreed anyone who wanted to pursue the project could do so and whoever got it done first and could assume the obligations would win.

Guest contacted McLaughlin and invited him to join in putting the deal together. McLaughlin agreed and he, Guest, and Stephens began an effort to secure financing in the latter part of 1983.

From the very beginning, the developers realized the ability to offer guests a complete package of amenities including boating, golf, and tennis would be key to the project's success both from the standpoint of acquiring financing as well as the hotel's ultimate operation once open. To accomplish this, they needed not only a lease for the submerged land in the yacht basin to build the marina, but also city-owned land adjacent to the hotel site where they wanted to build tennis courts.

The hotel had a one hundred-year lease on land behind the hotel that stretched from Fifth Avenue to about halfway between Sixth and Seventh Avenues and extending all the way to the water. The city wanted that piece of property so they could work on their waterfront park system. An exchange seemed the logical solution, but both the lease for the submerged land and the land swap required public referendums.

When this photo was taken, Fred Guest, the developer credited with saving the Vinoy, was dining in Fred's with Chris Evert, former president of the Women's Tennis Association.

Photo courtesy of Niles Laughner and Lois Laughner Sullivan

The citizens of St. Petersburg showed where their hearts were when it came to saving the Vinoy with their votes. That November, they approved the land exchange with a vote 72,692 to 22,798 and the lease of submerged land in the Vinoy yacht basin for seventy-four boat slips by a margin of 67,386 to 27,489.

The victory had its price. The developers gave the city ownership of the property now known as Vinoy Park. In addition, they agreed they would not erect any buildings on the eastern two hundred feet of their property plus the property they received. They were further limited in that they could not develop buildings for other than recreational purposes without a referendum. They also gave $60,000 to upgrade the landscaping of Vinoy Park. And the lease on the submerged land contained the proviso that the marina must be built within five years.

In 1987, Guest, McLaughlin, and Stephens formed the Vinoy Development Corporation and reached agreement with Alberding on a lease. The period from late 1983 until they were able to close a loan in February 1990, seemed a very long time from the standpoint of the city. The developers talked to representatives from countless hotels and lenders. Of that painful and interminable period, McLaughlin said, "I don't think there was a hotel company that does four or five star properties that we didn't talk to. Along the way, whenever a hotel company or a lender turned us down, we asked why and we listened."

What they heard was discouraging. They were told that St. Petersburg did not have the image of a progressive city. They were also told they were trying to do a four or five star resort in a downtown location, not on the beach. The inference, of course, was that it would never work. Nonetheless, they believed in their project and in the Vinoy so they persevered.

As time passed, they learned it would be necessary to make significant changes to the hotel's basic floor plan. The rooms that even Laughner considered small were virtually miniscule when compared to those being offered by more modern properties. "Historic properties have about 198 square feet of net living area which excludes entry, closet and bathroom. Today we are at around 310 to 360 square feet of net living area. The Vinoy did not come anywhere near today's standards," McLaughlin said.

The problem of size was further complicated because all of the Vinoy's rooms were interconnected and every room had one centered window. Ultimately, the expanded room size was accomplished without changing the facade by combining three rooms into two. And they turned one sideways so the each room would have two windows.

Then there was the Savings & Loan crisis.

During this period, interest rates soared to 20 percent and significant changes were made to the tax code. Prior to these changes, investors seeking a loss for tax purposes could take 98 percent of the loss as a tax deduction along with a small piece of the profits. Now developers of historic properties had to change the way they raised their equity.

At the same time, the financial community was battling to survive the savings and loan crisis, an issue with drastic ramifications for developers everywhere. The 1980s were not the logical time to be trying to finance a five-star resort in downtown St. Petersburg—especially prior to the Pier, the park, the Dome (now known as Tropicana Field) and the Mahaffey Theater being done.

Even after those projects were in the works, prospective lenders asked back for a second look at the Vinoy were leery. The widely held opinion was that downtown St. Petersburg held a lot of potential, but it was too early to be sure of the outcome. And always looming in the background like a black cloud was the possibility that the city would quit threatening and actually condemn the hotel before the developers could obtain financing.

The process of locating an investor was further complicated by the fact that every time potential lenders were brought into town for a site visit, they were contacted by the newspaper almost before they checked in. The Vinoy was a beloved property and the TIMES, even though behaving like a father interviewing prospective suitors for a daughter's hand, was actually just doing its job. In keeping the public up to date on what was happening, however, the paper's preliminary public exposure often created problems. It was not a time for men weak of heart or conviction.

However, not all was gloom and doom. The developers had support and help. "Every time we brought a potential lender here, Marty Normile, director of a downtown development organization, and Paul Getting, executive director of the Downtown Chamber of Commerce, would put together a tag team presentation on how progressive St. Petersburg was and how the median age of residents had fallen and they assembled kits containing positive, up to date economic data about the area," McLaughlin said.

OPPOSITE: In 1984 when this aerial photo was taken, the Vinoy was in sad condition. Years of decay and neglect lay ahead, but there would be a happy ending for the hotel everyone in St. Petersburg loved and called its Crown Jewel.

90

Another of the tag team players was Clarence (Mac) W. McKee, Jr., executive vice president and chief financial officer of Florida Progress, the holding company for the local electric utility. McKee not only spoke to potential lenders convincing them of community support, he made the Florida Progress helicopter available so that lenders could see the area from the air. And Bob Ulrich, then St. Petersburg mayor, was also a tremendous asset, helping assure the interested parties that there was political support. The enthusiasm of these civic stalwarts was relentless and not to be denied.

In late 1988, the developers approached Smith Barney. Fred Guest was well known and respected by the firm with the result that Smith Barney agreed to help put together equity investors for the project.

Guest and Stephens explained what they wanted in the way of management and Smith Barney responded that it had an equity player that was also involved in management—Stouffer Hotels and Resorts. Within a week, the developers had signed a letter of intent with Stouffer. They owned 72 percent of the partnership and Stouffer owned the remaining 28 percent. Work began in earnest on plans, market studies, and purchasing the property.

Both parties agreed the marina was extremely important to the success of the project. But time to build the marina was running out.

"Bill Hulett, president of Stouffer was an avid boater," McLaughlin said, "and that marina was the hook. Not only because of his interest, but because that marina would set the Vinoy apart from the others since we are not on the beach. We had to have the amenities—we wanted the marina, golf course, tennis complex. And Hulett and Stouffer would move forward—provided we could build the marina."

The extension of time required another referendum, but this one was different because the developers were opposed by one of the most powerful entities in the city—the newspaper. The ST. PETERSBURG TIMES urged people to vote no on the marina in 1989, taking the position that they didn't believe it was necessary. "Get the hotel done," they wrote, "and we believe the people will support you in getting the marina."

Realizing only too well that the newspaper's opposition could jeopardize the entire project, the developers counteracted the negative impact of the TIMES' campaign by hosting an open house the weekend before the referendum. They opened the Vinoy to the public from 10:00 AM till 5:00 PM on Saturday and noon till 5:00 PM Sunday. They ran only one ad, but the turnout during those twelve brief hours was both amazing and heartening. In those few hours, they handed out more than 21,000 flyers although more than twice that number of interested local people dropped by. The streets were so congested, the police had to direct traffic.

The developers left nothing to chance. The open house was an entertaining and informative event. They had photographs from the past and renderings of the future. Volunteers in straw hats shared memories and anecdotes about the resort and served cookies and lemonade. In what is now Marchand's, Stouffer personnel mounted the traveling display they sent to trade shows. Upstairs on the mezzanine, the developers created a colorful display with information about the marina.

Once again the citizens of St. Petersburg came through although it was a close call. In the general election held March 28, 1989, the voters approved Charter Amendment No. 3, Ordinance No. 1089-F, the amendment for leasing the submerged land in the Vinoy basin for seventy-four boat slips by a slim margin of 29,019 to 25,502 votes.

The referendum behind them, the developers moved forward retaining J. P. Morgan to help them place the debt. Morgan put together a prospectus informing lenders that if they didn't respond by the deadline and if their offer was not complete, if they didn't meet every term, their offer would not be considered.

"For us this was 'gulp time,'" McLaughlin recalls. "We had been going to lenders on bended knees. However, Nestle (Stouffer's parent company) had never defaulted on a loan and had a wonderful credit rating. That gave J. P. Morgan clout to deal with lenders and we dealt with only the top ten banks in the world."

OPPOSITE: While the construction of the 74-slip marina would prove one of the most contentious issues during the resort's restoration, the marina proved to be a vitally important addition to the Vinoy's amenities' package.

On February 22, 1990, the developers—after years of disappoint-ment and delays—closed on a $66 million construction loan from Barclays Bank PLC of England and Credit Lyonnais of France. They moved quickly to find a general contractor and in December 1989, the St. Petersburg-based Federal Construction Company was award-ed a $33.6 million contract to renovate and expand the Vinoy.

And now the work began in earnest. Federal personnel met with the developers, representatives from Stouffer and architect William Cox to inspect and analyze the site to determine exactly what had to be done to comply with current standards while retaining the neces-sary historic elements. It was not an easy project because Cox and Federal also had to comply with the latest safety regulations while keeping the modern improvements nearly invisible.

Finally, in May 1990, they began the demolition of unwanted walls and chimneys along with repairs to existing concrete columns, beams, lintels, and slabs. The Vinoy was tented for termites, the entire roof was replaced and more than five hundred windows were removed, inspected, and repaired.

Simultaneous progress continued on the amenities package. In early 1985, the developers had talked to Alberding who owned the Sunset Golf Course on Snell Island. Bert Stephens, who had known him a long time, explained it was absolutely essential that they have the golf course. Otherwise, the Vinoy would be unable to compete with other five-star resorts. Alberding agreed and they worked out the terms. They also knew that the course and the clubhouse would need a lot of work since neither had been properly maintained for a number of years. Golf course architect Ron Garl was contacted in Lakeland, Florida, to renovate the Sunset Golf Course and plans were drawn to redo the exterior of the clubhouse and to build a pro shop, locker rooms, restaurant, and swimming pool.

The developers turned their attention to tennis. They wanted to have several "Grand Slam" tennis surfaces to set the Vinoy apart from other resorts—red clay for the French Open, Har-Tru for U.S. and Australian Opens, and grass for Wimbledon.

Marty Normile had learned that the Women's Tennis Association was looking for a new home. With his assistance, they put together a proposal. The WTA board agreed and the Vinoy became their official headquarters. They planned to stage clinics, exhibitions, and matches on the hotel courts and now, with the passage of the refer-endum and the extension of time to build the marina, the amenities package was complete.

OPPOSITE
Top: This rendering provides an overview of the ambitious plans for the Vinoy's restoration including the marina, the tennis courts behind and to the right of the ballroom, the new pool, and the adjacent guestroom tower.

BOTTOM: Work was underway on the Vinoy's restoration in February 1991, when this photo was taken. It would be sixteen months and $93 million before the hotel would reopen.

Rendering courtesy of Federal Construction

TOP: The Vinoy's crest was being restored, and the entrance would be updated to provide an area where guests might park while their luggage was unpacked.

BOTTOM: The elegant lobby was a shell of what it would become when this photo was taken in the summer of 1991.

OPPOSITE

TOP: The restoration of the lobby was a major project, but the end result would evoke the opulence and elegance so evident at the original opening.

BOTTOM: One of the final projects was the completion of the pool shown here with the Esplanade in the back, the waterfall in the center, and the pool at the bottom.

OVERLEAF:

LEFT: Eight months later in October, progress had been made but much work lay ahead.

TOP RIGHT: Local artist Tom Stovall (shown here) and his two-man crew worked eight hours a day for three months—much of that time on their backs—restoring by hand the friezes, borders, and panels in the dining room. Stovall faced a formidable task because there had been extensive damage. He began by taking precise measurements, slides, and photographs of the room from every conceivable angle. In his studio, he recreated the original designs. Nine months later after the construction work had been completed, he walked back in and began work.

BOTTOM RIGHT: Tom Stovall and his crew had completed the frieze in the dining room, but major work remained to be done to meet the deadline.

96

Photo from the Renaissance Vinoy Resort Archives

Photo from the Renaissance Vinoy Resort Archives

Photo from the Renaissance Vinoy Resort Archives

Photo from the Renaissance Vinoy Resort Archives

Work continued throughout 1990, 1991, and well into the summer of 1992. As the restoration progressed, costs mounted, ultimately reaching $93 million, but the hotel gradually regained its elegance and beauty. No longer an eyesore, it became truly a symbol of downtown St. Petersburg's rebirth and the city rejoiced when the Vinoy reopened on Friday, July 31, 1992.

Just as in 1925, the staff worked till the last moment cleaning and preparing guest rooms. And there were mishaps. Bed spreads and skirts ordered for the king-size beds were too short and replacements hadn't arrived until Tuesday and Wednesday. Crews hired to place furniture, hang pictures, and arrange accessories worked till midnight. Only 200 of the 360 rooms were ready for guests and some of those were not completely finished, but after being closed for seventeen long years, the Vinoy once again opened and on time.

Photo courtesy of Tom Stovall

Photo from the Renaissance Vinoy Resort Archives

99

TOP: By July 1, 1992, when this photo was taken, the grand reopening was a mere thirty days away.

BOTTOM: Restored to its original splendor, the ballroom was ready and waiting for diners on the happy occasion of the Vinoy's grand reopening on July 31, 1992.

OPPOSITE

TOP: The countdown was on and the grand reopening was mere hours away when this photo was taken in the lobby by the ST. PETERSBURG TIMES. At 4:40 PM Thursday, word came over the public address system that the Vinoy had received its certificate of occupancy. Although workers cheered, no one quit work—they were still unpacking boxes of lamps, installing wooden handrails in the ballroom, testing the fountains, and putting the finishing touches on the portecochere at the entrance.

BOTTOM: Made it! By July 31, 1992, the dining room was completed and staffed. The dining room contains both Marchand's Bar and Grill and The Terrace Room. Marchand's features Mediterranean cuisine with an emphasis on roasting, grilling and sautéing using fresh herbs and olive oil. The Terrace Room, with its impressive pillars, intricate plaster carvings, hand-painted ceiling and walls has a menu which features seafood and creative pasta. Guests have additional choices including Alfresco, the resort's Florida-style restaurant overlooking the pool. Both the ambience and the menu are tropical. Or there's Fred's Bar, named after Fred Guest. This elegant private dining room is open only to Vinoy Club members and resort guests. The cuisine is continental and features steaks and fresh seafood. Golfers enjoy the more casual cuisine offered by the Clubhouse Restaurant at the Vinoy at the Vinoy Golf Club.

Photo from the Renaissance Vinoy Resort Archives

Photo from the Renaissance Vinoy Resort Archives

Photo courtesy of the St. Petersburg Times

Photo from the Renaissance Vinoy Resort Archives

101

"At 2:00 PM Friday, pianist Natalya Danilov swung into RHAPSODY IN BLUE (music played at the hotel's grand opening New Year's Eve 1925) in the lobby of the Stouffer Vinoy Resort," wrote ST. PETERSBURG TIMES Staff Writer Judy Stark. "The first guests sipped their complimentary glasses of Aymer's Promenade Punch, the house cocktail. In the forecourt, valets leaped to open doors and unload luggage. It could have been 1925 all over again."

Earlier that morning, Aymer Laughner's son Paul and Pam Shriver, president of the Women's Tennis Association, became the first guests to register in the newly reopened resort. A little later, Laughner stepped to the podium in the ballroom and told an audience of a hundred or so friends and elected officials, "I wish to God he (his father) was here to see it. He built this hotel because he loved St. Petersburg. It's going to do well."

On hand for the opening were his wife, Lois, and their children, Sandy, Niles who worked on the resort's activities staff, Lynda and her husband, Werner Kohlenberg, and Vinoy, his wife, Patrice, and their daughter Elice.

"Thank you, thank you, thank you," said St. Petersburg Mayor Dave Fischer. "We thank you for getting us out of the frustrating dilemma we watched for 15 years."

And so the Vinoy was once again open. The main difference was that the beautiful hotel, poised like a crown jewel on St. Petersburg's waterfront, would be open year-round. And her guests although still among the affluent, storied names of today, would stay a matter of days, perhaps a week or so rather than the entire

LEFT: The reopening was an elegant occasion filled with new excitement and old memories. In this photo, Pam Shriver, left, president of the Women's Tennis Association, and Paul Laughner, son of Aymer Vinoy Laughner, registered as the first guests of the newly reopened Vinoy.

RIGHT: The event was the Vinoy's seventieth anniversary and champagne was the order of the evening. Partygoers danced to the music of the Paul Whiteman Orchestra, just as they had in 1925. As a special treat Robert Gourdin, Master Saber with Moet & Chandon champagne, opened several bottles with only a saber in traditional Russian Hussar style.

OPPOSITE: The night of the grand reopening, July 31, 1992, the beautifully restored Vinoy Resort was ablaze with light. In the months and years ahead, it would fulfill its promise winning a number of the hospitality industry's most prestigious awards including the Mobil Four Star rating, the AAA Four Diamond Award, Zagat's Travel Excellence Award, the Aster Award, the Award of Excellence, the Pinnacle Award, the Gold Key Award, the Paragon Award, and in 1998 was named to CONDÉ NAST TRAVELER magazine's Gold List which ranks the world's leading hotels, resorts, spas, and cruise lines. Upon reopening in 1992 the Renaissance Vinoy was listed as a member of the Historic Hotels of America, one of only four in Florida and seventy-five nationwide. There are currently one hundred forty-five members nationwide.

103

WINE LIST
Champagne and Sparkling Wines
Moet & Chandon, White Star, Epernay
48.00
Schramsberg, Blanc de Blanc, N~
36.00

Original I

STOUFFER VINOY RESORT
SPECIAL PREVIEW EVENING

MENU
Crab and Shrimp Cocktail with Mango
and Citrus Vinaigrette
or
Tortellini with Four Cheeses
Oven–dried Tomatoes
***
Mixed Field Greens, Basil Vinaigrette
and Grilled Rye
***
Grilled Thai Style Swordfish with
Buckwheat Noodles and Citrus Butter
or
Pepper Crusted Roast Loin of Beef
with Rosemary Potatoes
or
Chicken Breast, Braised Leeks
and CousCous
***
Warm Apple Tarte with Almond
Creme Anglaise
or
Flourless Chocolate Torte with
Cinnamon Ice Cream
***
Coffee, Decaffeinated Coffee
and Specialty Teas

Friday, July 31, 1992

Menu from the Renaissance Vinoy Resort Archives

TOP: The menu for the grand reopening, shown here, duplicated the menu used during the 1950–1951 season and featured area seafood and citrus.

BOTTOM: Executive Chef Tom Chin (center), assisted by his executive staff, is responsible for all aspects of food service including the five restaurants and lounges, full catering services for functions in the ballrooms, pavilion, Tea Garden, and Esplanade, 24-hour room service and poolside service.

Photo from the Renaissance Vinoy Resort Archives

season. Other than these and the natural changes time always brings, it was business as usual.

The months and years ahead would not be without their problems. Business that first year after the reopening was slow. Occupancy was less than 45 percent, a fact that had little to do with the resort and its management and more to do with the fact that it would take time to reinstate and reposition the hotel as a contender in the now extremely competitive hospitality industry. Additionally, the hotel industry suffered through a recession in the early 1990s. Despite these setbacks, the hotel's occupancy had increased in 65 percent in 1995 and would have been profitable had it not been for these factors along with the heavy debt load.

In July 1993, less than a year after its reopening, the Vinoy was forced into foreclosure. This time, however, the hotel remained open, occupancy continued to increase and in January of 1996, the hotel was purchased by the Renaissance Hotel Group which is headquartered in Hong Kong.

Photo from the Renaissance Vinoy Resort Archives

TO REOPEN THE VINOY IN 1992, IT REQUIRED:

34,000 yards of carpet
10,000 yards of upholstery
17,000 yards of draperies
66,000 pieces of silver, china and glassware
including more than 17,000 glasses
864 chrome salt and pepper sets
8,700 washcloths
6,000 hand towels
1,400 bath mats
5,600 king-size sheets
6,000 pillowcases
more than 1,000 pillows
2,200 bathrobes

Photo from the Renaissance Vinoy Resort Archives

THE HAPPY ENDING

As the millennium approaches, the Renaissance Vinoy stands poised on St. Petersburg's bustling waterfront, ready for 2000 and the years beyond. Occupancy has climbed to better than 75 percent and construction of a $10 million dollar conference center/ballroom has strengthened her position. She has survived and is a prime example of "the revival of the fittest" as one magazine dubbed her rebirth. She is a symbol not only of the beauty and elegance of another age, but of the devotion of her community. In a sense, she is also a memorial to the men who loved and owned her, the men who would not give up, the men who persisted against all odds until they experienced the joy of seeing her saved and seeing her doors once more open wide in welcome.

PALM COURT BALLROOM—RENAISSANCE VINOY RESORT

Photo courtesy of the Renaissance Vinoy Resort Archives

LEFT: The future is bright. The Palm Court Ballroom which will provide additional space for special events and meetings will be opening in 2000.

OPPOSITE: Timeless beauty is reflected in the architectural detail of this restored window in the Vinoy's main dining room.

THE HISTORY OF THE
VINOY RESORT GOLF
AND COUNTRY CLUB

N 1920, AS C. Perry Snell began constructing the clubhouse of his Coffee Pot Golf Course, (named after Coffee Pot Bayou where it's located), World War I had been over for little more than a year. St. Petersburg was a city in transition, stirring awake to find itself on the verge of the real estate boom. Tourism was becoming an important industry and recognized as such by community leaders. Voters had just elected the first woman, Virginia Burnside, to the city council and, equally as significant, women had helped elect her. Although women elsewhere in the nation would not win the right to vote until the adoption of the Nineteenth Amendment in August 1920, St. Petersburg women had won that right in a referendum held in July 1919. That same year, the city spent an incredible $12 million to build paved roads, but the expenditure wasn't an extravagance because St. Petersburg was truly a city on the move.

PREVIOUS SPREAD: Renaissance Vinoy Resort Golf Course with clubhouse in the background.

RIGHT AND OPPOSITE: The Sunset Golf Club on Snell Isle was the brainchild of C. Perry Snell. Even when the Great Depression crushed the real estate market, Snell refused to relinquish his dream and persisted in developing Snell Isle. Later, he sold the golf club to the Clark family, who painted a replica of the orange and blue Clark candy bar wrapper on the tower.

Photo from the Renaissance Vinoy Resort Archives

110

And no one was more aware of that than Snell who was creating a nine-hole golf course for the affluent winter residents who would be buying the upscale homes in his development on Snell Island. Local lore has it that Donald Ross designed that first golf course and, although documentation has never been uncovered to prove it, Ross probably did. He was already well established as the dean of American golf course designers, he had done golf courses literally all over Florida including the Belleview Biltmore in nearby Clearwater and in 1920, there just weren't that many fine golf course designers.

The original clubhouse which displayed a subtle Japanese influence was replaced in 1925–1926. The second clubhouse, once dubbed the local Taj Mahal, was reportedly a section of a palace Snell bought overseas and had reconstructed on its present site. It was Moorish in design, featuring minarets, heavily bracketed cornices, keyhole arches, and onion domes as well as adages inscribed in a form of Arabic in the masonry walls. Seen through the second entrance door in the ballroom were the words, "With your prophets

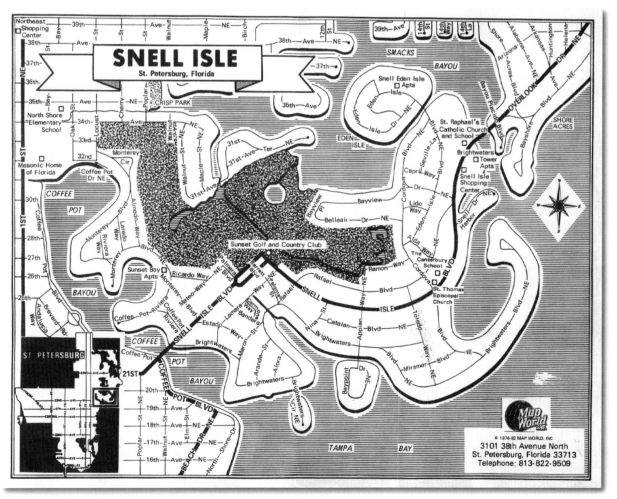

Map from the Renaissance Vinoy Resort Archives

TOP: According to local lore, the clubhouse, shown here circa 1932, was once a section of a European palace brought to St. Petersburg and reconstructed in 1926, when only 39 acres of 278-acre Snell Island were above high tide.

MIDDLE: The dining room at the Sunset Golf Club was designed and decorated as a replica of a Middleastern mosque and open air market, complete with the requisite keyhole arches, inlaid tile, and Arabic inscriptions, as well as a 5,300-square-foot ballroom.

BOTTOM: The roof of the original ballroom at the Sunset Golf Club could be rolled back so performers and guests could enjoy the sun as well as the stars. In this photo, a ballerina intrigued the crowd with her performance.

OPPOSITE: In 1948 Alberding purchased the Sunset Golf and Country Club, which was only a mile from the hotel entrance. Guests were welcome to play there and transportation to and from the 6,116-yard course was provided by the hotel.

the world." Outside and above one of the windows was written what is loosely translated as, "No god but God and there is no winner but him." And above the entrance door appeared the words, "King of the World."

The roof of the ballroom was designed so that it could be rolled back allowing dancers to see the evening sky while they pirouetted across the floor. The interior was filled with statuary Snell had brought from Europe. In his enthusiasm, Snell also scattered the elegant statuary in strategic positions around the golf course. These were later removed because they created hazards when less than proficient duffers sliced balls that caromed off statues striking other golfers.

When Snell sold the golf course and twenty-four lots on Snell Island to the Clark Company in 1932, the Clark family changed the name to the Sunset Golf and Country Club, put in a water tower on which they painted an orange and blue Clark Candy Bar, added to the clubhouse putting in a kitchen and hired local golfer E. P. "Bill" Cody as manager.

Photo from the Renaissance Vinoy Resort Archives

Management during the Clark ownership was unorthodox, to say the least. According to Elmer Henneka who joined the club in 1940, no two members paid the same price for a membership. He's quoted as saying, "It was just whatever the management thought would be interesting enough to keep some playing there."

In 1948, the Alsonett Hotel chain bought the golf course and in November 1949 engaged William R. Watts in to manage the club. Under his leadership, tennis courts were added along with a modern swimming pool and a pro shop to replace the original pro shop which was destroyed by fire in 1958.

Just as women played a prominent role in St. Petersburg when the golf course was first built, they played an important part in the golf course's history. In 1953 professional golfer Babe Zaharias, who owned a golf course in Tampa, approached the St. Petersburg Chamber of Commerce with the idea of holding a Professional Golf Women's Open. Zaharias, Watts, and Ed Turville, chairman of the Chamber Sports Committee, convinced City Manager Ross Windom and the city of St. Petersburg to guarantee the purse.

That first tournament, the Women's Golf Open, was one of the first tournaments on the Ladies Professional Golf Association's tour. Participants consisted of eighteen professionals and two hundred

RIGHT: Famous woman golfer Marilyn Smith is shown at the Sunset Golf Course and Country club with the 1967 trophy for the St. Petersburg Women's Open Golf Tournament. In 1953, world-renowned woman athlete Babe Zaharias Didrikson who owned a golf course in Tampa approached the Chamber of Commerce with the idea of starting a Professional Golf Women's Open. Ed Turville, chairman of the Chamber's sports committee, got the city of St. Petersburg to guarantee the purse.

OPPOSITE: This group of professional women golfers posed with their trophies following the St. Petersburg Women's Open Golf Championship held April 1, 1964, at the Sunset Golf and Country Club. The name of the tournament was changed in 1968 to the Orange Blossom Open and in 1980 to the S & H Golf Classic.

Photo from the Renaissance Vinoy Resort Archives

amateurs. The roster of professionals included stellar women golfers including Zaharias, Louise Suggs, Patty Berg, and Beverly Hansen. Hansen won in sudden death, defeating Zaharias on the third hole of the playoff.

In 1963, Lynn Andrews, who had succeeded Windom as city manager, told Watts the city would no longer sponsor the event and asked Watts to organized a group to continue the tournament. Watts, George B. MacCurry, Billy Belcher, and L. W. Baynard, Sr., and a group of friends formed a corporation called St. Petersburg Women's Open Golf Championship, Inc., on March 4, 1964.

MacCurry, then president of the corporation, felt the men who operated the tournament should have a name. Charles W. Mackey conceived the name Polywog by combining poly, a Greek prefix meaning many, with the acronym wog standing for women's open golf.

On January 2, 1968, the name of the corporation was changed to Orange Blossom Open, Inc. The tournament's name was changed to the Orange Blossom Open and in 1980 to the S & H Golf Classic. In 1990, the Polywogs entered a new era of tournament sponsorship—the Orange Blossom Classic Pro-Am which has raised hundreds of thousands of dollars for local charities.

Photo from the Renaissance Vinoy Resort Archives

Photo from the Renaissance Vinoy Resort Archives

When developers Fred Guest, Bert Stephens, and Craig McLaughlin were attempting to reopen the Vinoy, they approached Charles Alberding whose Alsonett chain owned the golf course and negotiated a one hundred-year lease on the course and the clubhouse.

The first phase of the course's $9 million renovation was completed in time for the reopening in 1992, but it would take five years and an additional $1 million before the interior of the clubhouse was completed. The reopening on September 14, 1997, was a happy event for the community.

The Renaissance Vinoy Resort gave the Snell Isle Foundation the opportunity to hold St. Petersburg's first social event in the newly refurbished structure. The event was a cocktail-buffet with the money raised to be used by the Foundation for the beautification of city parks and parkways on Snell Island. It was, according to all reports, a smashing success. Celebrants gathered in the opulent Sunset Ballroom which was decorated in a Mediterranean theme similar to the grand ballroom at the resort. They toured the other rooms in the clubhouse including the Polywog Room which has an original carved fireplace depicting cherubs playing in the heavens.

Like the Renaissance Vinoy, the golf course has survived both time and change and although it was not St. Petersburg's first golf course, it is today the city's oldest.

OPPOSITE: Golf-course architect Ron Garl, the designer responsible for at least nine of the top fifty courses in Florida, was chosen to renovate the Sunset Golf Course. The course, completed in time for the grand reopening, is an 18-hole par-70 championship course constructed to have an old-world feel reminiscent of the St. Andrew's course in Scotland because of its double greens and the way the course plays. That first phase also included the golf course, the clubhouse exterior, the pro shop, locker rooms, and restaurant as well as the swimming pool. Painstaking care was taken to preserve and protect the environment during the renovation. The $9 million project was well underway in January of 1992 when this photo was taken. The course has since received the Golden Links Award, the Florida Nursery Growers Association of Excellence Award, the Environmental Excellence Award, and the Greens of Distinction Award.

LEFT: In 1990, the Sunset Golf and Country Club became part of the plans for the grand reopening of the Renaissance Vinoy Resort and, in 1997, the clubhouse was reopened having been restored to its original beauty.

Photo from the Renaissance Vinoy Resort Archives

117

TOP LEFT: In 1996, celebrity fashion commentator Mr. Blackwell, famous for his Worst Dressed Lists, inscribed his photo, "For the Vinoy, a really 'Terrific' Home away from Home. I'll be back."

TOP RIGHT: In January 1995, Dan Rather anchored the CBS EVENING NEWS from the Esplanade at the Vinoy. His visit was to help promote WTSP, Channel 10 as the new CBS affiliate.

BOTTOM LEFT: Broadcaster Paul Harvey graciously posed for photographers during his stay at the Vinoy in 1994.

BOTTOM RIGHT: General Norman Schwartzkopf was another distinguished guest, in town to be interviewed by Dan Rather on the CBS EVENING NEWS.

OPPOSITE:
TOP: Former President and Mrs. Bush visited the Vinoy in early 1995, pausing to shake hands with Executive Chef Tom Chin after dining in the Alfresco restaurant. President Jimmy Carter and his wife, Rosalyn, have stayed at the Vinoy as well as Elizabeth Dole.

MIDDLE: Musician and composer Yanni obligingly posed during a stay at the Vinoy in 1998. Renowned tenor Luciano Pavarotti also stayed at the Vinoy. Pavarotti instructed the staff that he would cook all his own meals in his room entailing the purchase and installation of a full-size refrigerator, pots and pans, a portable gas cooker, and a 100-plus item grocery list in his suite. It was extra work, but service has always been the very essence of the Vinoy's philosophy.

BOTTOM: Vice President and Mrs. Al Gore stayed at the Vinoy during the Vice Presidential debates in October 1996. While there, they took time to pose with their children for their 1996 Christmas card. Tipper Gore also paused from her busy schedule long enough to have her photo taken with members of the Vinoy staff.

Photo from the Renaissance Vinoy Resort Archives

Photo from the Renaissance Vinoy Resort Archives

Photo from the Renaissance Vinoy Resort Archives

Photo from the Renaissance Vinoy Resort Archives

Photo from the Renaissance Vinoy Resort Archives

Photo from the Renaissance Vinoy Resort Archives

Photo from the Renaissance Vinoy Resort Archives

In 1992, The Vinoy Club, a private members resort club, was created. This Club provides local residents the opportunity to join the club and utilize the Resort amenities, including Health Club, Swimming Pools, Tennis Courts, Golf Course, Marina, and a private dining room "Fred's Bar," named after Fred Guest. As of today, The Vinoy Club has over 1,000 memberships. These members are an active, integral part of the success of the Resort today.

Mr. and Mrs. Stephen Abelman (Helene)
Mr. and Mrs. Peter Abraham (Vera)
Mr. and Mrs. Allan Adams (Lynn)
Mr. and Mrs. Harvey Adams (Cheryl)
Mr. Payton Adams
Ms. Christine Agee
Col. and Mrs. Bill Alden (M. Anne)
Mr. and Mrs. E. J. Alderson (Eleanor)
Mr. and Mrs. Anthony Alesi (Susan)
Mr. and Mrs. David Allen (Linda)
Ms. Margaret Allison
Mr. and Mrs. Alan Almengual (Kathryn)
Dr. and Mrs. Edward Amley (Margaret)
Dr. and Mrs. Robert Amley (Roberta)
Mr. Allen Anderson
Ms. Sally Anderson
Mr. and Mrs. Steve Anderson (Anne)
Ms. Terri Anderson
Mr. and Mrs. Lynn Andrews (Jane)
Drs. Tom and Jennifer Andrews
Mr. and Mrs. Wayne Andrews (Barbara)
Mr. Stewart Angel
Mr. Charles Angell
Mr. and Mrs. Jerry Angelo (Bernadette)
Mr. and Mrs. Judy Appelbaum (Roy)
Mr. and Mrs. Robert Apple (Lisa)
Drs. Peter and Mary Linda Armacost
Mr. and Mrs. James Armour (Maryann)
Mr. Kenneth Armstrong
Mr. Laurence Arnold
Mrs. and Mrs. Craig Ascari (Jean)
Mr. and Mrs. Alexander Astrack (Cynthia)
Mr. and Mrs. William Atchley, Jr. (Sally)
Mr. and Mrs. David Atha (Helene)
Mr. Dustin Atkatz
Mrs. Noreen Atkatz
Mr. Barry Augenbraun
Mr. Richard Avis and Dr. Victoria Woods
Dr. and Mrs. Roy Babcock (Suzanne)
Mr. and Mrs. William Bachschmidt (Debora)
Mr. Kenneth Bagot and Anne Sweazey
Mr. and Mrs. James Baker (Patricia)
Mr. Thomas Balkan
Mr. and Mrs. Charlie Banks (Judy)
Dr. and Mrs. Greg Baran (Cynthia)
Dr. and Mrs. Jerry Barbosa (Carol)
Mr. Guntis Barenis
Mr. and Mrs. Michael Barger (Joan)
Mr. and Mrs. Brian Barker (Lynn)
Ms. Claudia Barleon
Mr. E. Scott Barlow
Mr. Andrew Barnes
Mr. and Mrs. Scott Barnes (Grace)
Dr. John Barnett
Mr. and Mrs. Robert Barnett (Karen)
Mr. and Mrs. Joseph Bartholomew

Mr. B. J. Barwick, Jr.
Mr. and Mrs. Giles Bax (Patricia)
Ms. Lisa Ann Bayer
Ms. Fay Baynard
Mr. and Mrs. William Baynard, Jr.
Mr. William Baynard, Sr.
Mr. and Mrs. Brad Baytos (Dana)
Mr. and Mrs. Douglas Beairsto (Murray)
Dr. Susan Beaven
Mr. and Mrs. Charles Beck (Ruth)
Mr. Jim Belcher
Mrs. Margaret Benedetti
Dr. and Mrs. Michael Benedict (Betsy)
Mr. and Mrs. David Berg (Dana)
Ms. Penelope Berg
Col. and Mrs. Robert Berns (Suzanne)
Mr. Robert Berra
Mr. James Berry
Mr. and Mrs. James Berry
Mr. and Mrs. John Berry (Nancy)
Mr. George Biaouette
Mr. and Mrs. Richard Bible (Carrie)
Mr. and Mrs. Roy Binger (Angela)
Ms. Lorraine Bird
Dr. Vance Bishop
Mr. and Mrs. Charles Bissett (Ruth)
Mr. and Mrs. Neal Blackburn (Sandy)
Mr. and Mrs. Worth Blackwell (Elizabeth)
Mr. John Blackwood
Dr. Richard Blanchard
Mr. and Mrs. William Blizzard (Patricia)
Mr. and Mrs. Roger Block (Victoria)
Mr. and Mrs. Delbert Bloss, Jr. (Daryl)
Mr. Ted Bodtmann
Ms. Amy Bofman
Mr. and Mrs. Brett Bolhofner (Janis)
Dr. and Mrs. Alfred Bonati (Patricia)
Mr. and Mrs. Tony Bond (Carolyn)
Mr. and Mrs. Wayne Bond (Jean)
Mr. and Mrs. William Bond, Jr. (Mary Ann)
Mr. William Bond, Sr.
Mr. and Mrs. Dennis Bongers (Mary Ann)
Dr. and Mrs. Luis Botero (Margarita)
Mr. and Mrs. Frank Boudinot (Elaine)
Dr. and Mrs. Joseph Boulay, Jr. (Suzanne)
Mr. and Mrs. Lynn Bourquardez (Sandra)
Dr. and Mrs. Richard Bower (Carolyn)
Mr. Jerry Bowles
Ms. Nancy Boyce
Dr. and Mrs. Dale Brandt (Sandy)
Mr. and Mrs. Rodney Brazzell (Gail)
Mr. and Mrs. David Bresler (Sheila)
Mr. and Mrs. Terrence Brett (Kim)
Ms. Donna Brewer
Mr. and Mrs. Greg Brewer (Sherry)
Mr. and Mrs. James Brice (Sandra)
Mr. and Mrs. John Bridge (Ann)
Mr. and Mrs. Dale Bridges (Leslie)
Mr. and Mrs. Terry Brimmer (Susan)
Mr. Thomas Brinkman
Mr. and Mrs. Mark Brody (Sue)
Mr. and Mrs. Jeffrey Brooks (Shirley)
Ms. Deborah Brown
Mr. Jeffrey Brown and Teresa Ross
Mr. Leehland Brown
Mr. Edward Brownstein
Ms. Carolyn Bruce
Mr. Charles Brumfield
Mr. and Mrs. Kenneth Bryant (Nancy)
Mr. and Mrs. Matthew Bryant (Laura)
Mr. and Mrs. Timothy Bryant (Mary)
Ms. Laurie Burcaw
Mr. James Burgess and Lee Silbert

Mr. and Mrs. Phillip Burgess (Nancy)
Mr. and Mrs. Thomas Burgess (Caron)
Mr. and Mrs. John Burket (Denise)
Dr. and Mrs. F. Joseph Burns (Joye)
Mr. and Mrs. Peter Bursik (Merribeth)
Mr. Rutland Bussey
Ms. Sherri Butler
Ms. Suzie Butts
Ms. Wilda Bynum
Mr. and Mrs. Ronald Caffrey (Kathleen)
Mr. and Mrs. Jack Cairl (Lois)
Mr. and Mrs. David Calametti (Jackie)
Mr. and Mrs. Peter Cammick (Vivian)
Mr. and Mrs. George Campbell (Pamela)
Mr. and Mrs. Robert Campbell (Tracey)
Mr. and Mrs. Philip Campbell, Jr. (Lucille)
Mr. Tom Canavan
Mr. and Mrs. James Canino (June)
Mr. and Mrs. Frank Carella (Petty)
Mr. and Mrs. Bill Carlisle (Mary Beth)
Dr. and Mrs. Jeffrey Carlson (Cheryl)
Mr. and Mrs. Vincent Caronongan (Donna)
Mr. Matt Carroll
Mr. Roy Carter
Dr. and Mrs. James Cashon (Rachel)
Dr. Dennis Cassidy and Suzanne Pileggi
Ms. Patricia Cassidy
Msgr. James Caverly
Mr. and Mrs. Emmanuel Cerf (Shelley)
Mr. and Mrs. rian Cesare (Dawn)
Ms. Magella Champagne
Mr. and Mrs. Robert Chapman (Karen)
Mr. and Mrs. F. Kneeland Chase (Susan)
Mr. Tom Chasm
Mr. and Mrs. Gerry Chastelet (Wendy)
Mr. Alex Cheung
Ms. Shelley Chew
Mr. and Mrs. Jorge G. Chiappo (Holle)
Mr. Louis Chipparoni
Mr. and Mrs. George Chism (Pat)
Mr. Mark Chmielewski and Linda Jantschek
Dr. and Mrs. John Chulick, Jr. (Patricia)
Dr. and Mrs. John Chulick, Sr. (Frances)
Mr. David Church
Mr. and Mrs. Robert Churuti (Susan)
Mr. Joseph Cillo
Mr. Dirk Cimarik and Sharon Vineyard
Mr. and Mrs. John Cissna (Lynn)
Mr. Robert Clampitt
Mr. and Mrs. Robert Clark (Lisa)
Dr. and Mrs. Bushnell Clarke (Susan)
Mr. and Mrs. Rueben Clarson (Elaine)
Mr. and Mrs. Kevin Clayton (Michelle)
Ms. Elizabeth Clemmer
Mr. Scott Clendening
Mr. Budd Cobb
Mr. and Mrs. William T. Cobb, Jr. (Catherine)
Dr. and Mrs. William Cobb (Terry)
Mr. and Mrs. Andrew Coch (Darlene)
Mr. and Mrs. David Cohen (Maureen)
Mr. and Mrs. James Cohen (Whitney)
Mr. Harry Collins
Dr. and Mrs. Paul S. Collins (Cathy)
Mr. and Mrs. Phil Collins (Melanie)
Mr. and Mrs. Gene Collins, Jr. (Barbara)
Ms. Pat Conant
Ms. Kathleen Condon
Dr. and Mrs. Ludner Confident (Marie)
Mr. and Mrs. Dominic Connelly (Susan)
Mr. and Mrs. Martin Conner, Sr. (Audrey)
Mr. Michael Conway

Mr. and Mrs. Tim Conway (Julia)
Mr. and Mrs. Clifford Cook (Margaretta)
Mr. Miller Cooper and Keri Allen-Cooper
Mr. and Mrs. Frank Cooper, Jr. (Grace)
Mr. and Mrs. Alfred Corey, Jr. (Antoinette)
Ms. SueAnn Corrigan
Mr. and Mrs. Milton Corson, Jr. (Deborah)
Mr. and Mrs. Andrew Corty (Betty)
Dr. and Mrs. Henry Cotman (Jacqueline)
Mr. and Mrs. Kevin Cottrill (Mandy)
Dr. and Mrs. Andrew Coundouriotis (Elaina)
Ms. Sharon Cowan
Mr. and Mrs. Les Craft (Susie)
Mr. and Mrs. James Craig (Barbara)
Dr. and Mrs. Joseph Craig (Carol)
Mr. and Mrs. Scott Crandall (Donna Ann)
Mr. and Mrs. Dale Cravey (Lynn)
Dr. Bruce Crawford
Mr. Rick Crawford
Ms. Candice Cray
Mr. Gayle Creel
Mr. Jose Crespi
Drs. Wade and Joanne Cressman
Ms. Christine Crosby
Mr. and Mrs. Troy Crotts (Lori)
Mr. and Mrs. James Cunneen (Cristina)
Ms. Jane Cunneen
Mr. August Curcio
Mr. and Mrs. Kevin Cureton (Betty)
Mr. and Mrs. Timothy Curran (Nancy)
Ms. Kimberly Curtis
Mr. and Mrs. Ward Curtis (Barbara)
Mr. and Mrs. Lisa D'Alessandro (Kurt)
Mr. and Mrs. Leo DAlton (Monica)
Mr. and Mrs. Michael Daniels (Amy)
Mr. Edward Dantini
Mrs. Elizabeth Dantini
Mr. and Mrs. John DaSilva (Alison)
Dr. Christopher Davey
Ms. Linda Davey
Mr. and Mrs. Chip Davis
Ms. Joann Davis
Ms. Tommy Davis
Ms. Anne Dawson
Dr. and Mrs. Peter Dawson (Jodie)
Mr. and Mrs. Louis de la Parte (Kim)
Ms. Daryl DeBerry and William Coffman
Mr. and Mrs. Robert Decker (Carol)
Mr. and Mrs. Steven Deininger (Barbara)
Mr. and Mrs. John Dennis, Jr. (Barbara)
Mr. and Mrs. Bruce Denson (Lynn)
Dr. and Mrs. Robert Dickerson (Kari)
Mr. Michael DiGirolamo
Ms. Alona Dishy
Mr. and Mrs. Craig Dobbin (Elaine)
Mr. and Mrs. John Domeier (Denise)
Mr. and Mrs. Robert Donaldson (Pam)
Mr. and Mrs. Vincent Dotolo (Connie)
Mr. Jeffrey Doty
Mr. and Mrs. William Dougherty (Sue)
Mr. and Mrs. Paul Douglass (Margie)
Mr. and Mrs. Fred Doyle (Laurie)
Mr. and Mrs. Daniel Doyle, Jr. (Nicole)
Rev. and Mrs. Walter Draughon III (Jane)
Dr. and Mrs. Gary Dresden (Trudy)
Mr. and Mrs. Joseph Dudek (Pauline)
Mr. and Mrs. Steven Duann (Jill)
Mr. and Mrs. Nga Duong (Xuan)
Dr. and Mrs. Glen DuPont (Janet)
Mr. and Mrs. Manual Duran (Gloria)
Mr. James Durning

Col. and Mrs. G. Thurman Dwyre
  (Leslie)
Mr. and Mrs. David Dyer (Harriet)
Ms. Alice Eachus
Mr. and Mrs. March Earle (Meg)
Mr. and Mrs. Richard EArle, III (Shirley)
Mr. Richard Early
Mr. P. R. Easterlin, Jr.
Ms. Christine Eaton
Mr. Sherri Ebelke
Mr. and Mrs. Richard Edmonds
  (Marianne)
Mr. William Edwards
Dr. and Mrs. Thomas Egan (Colleen)
Mr. Raymond Eichhof
Mr. Donnie Eliason, Jr.
Dr. and Mrs. John Elinger (Suzie)
Mr. Marvel Elliott
Mr. Max V. Elson
Mr. William C. Ely
Mr. William T. Ely
Ms. Jill N. Emery
Mr. and Mrs. Glen Epley (Mary)
Mr. and Mrs. Alfred Ernst, Jr. (Sandra)
Mr. and Mrs. Dwight Ervin (Wendi)
Mrs. Judy Estren and Richard Estren
Dr. and Mrs. Bill Evans (Melody)
Ms. Deborah Evans
Mr. and Mrs. Gregory Evans (Kathleen)
Dr. and Mrs. Perry Everett (Lisa)
Mr. Brian Everhart (Melissa)
Mr. Harry Evertz, III
Mr. Dan Evins
Mr. John Faile, Sr.
Dr. and Mrs. Frank Farkas (Toni Lee)
Mr. John Farmer
Mr. and Mrs. John Farrell (Tina)
Mr. and Mrs. David Feaster (Marcia)
Mr. and Mrs. David Feinberg (Helen)
Mr. and Mrs. Christopher Ferguson
  (Luanne)
Mr. and Mrs. Antonio Fernandez
  (Madelaine)
Mr. and Mrs. Bill Ferris (Mary (Bo)
Mr. and Mrs. Richard Finan (Alice)
Ms. Jayne Fiocca
Mayor and Mrs. David Fischer (Margo)
Mr. and Mrs. Ben Fisher (Carol)
Mr. Jacob Fisher
Mr. and Mrs. Gordon Fitzpatrick (Krista)
Mr. and Mrs. Hermann Flachsmann
  (Betty)
Dr. and Mrs. Thomas Flanagan (Jeri)
Mr. and Mrs. George Flatley (Lucy)
Mr. and Mrs. Joseph Fleece (Joanne)
Mr. and Mrs. James Fleming (Betsy)
Ms. Joanne James Fleming
Mr. Lucas Fleming
Ms. Mary Fletcher
Dr. and Mrs. John Flint (Frances)
Mr. and Mrs. Terry Fluke (Stephanie)
Ms. Marion Foelgner
Mr. and Mrs. Bruce Foltz (Mary Kay)
Ms. Carol Fontaine
Mr. David Ford and Kellyann Croghan
Mr. Robert Forlizzo
Dr. and Mrs. George Forster (Regina)
Mr. and Mrs. James Foster (Audrey)
Mr. and Mrs. Jeffrey Foster (Tamera)
Mr. Harrison Fox
Mr. and Mrs. Frank Fox, IV (Vicki)
Mr. Robert Francis
Mr. Erskine Franklin
Mr. and Mrs. Lee Frazier (Eleanor)
Mr. Robert Freihofer, Jr.
Mr. and Mrs. Janice French (Andrew)

Ms. Ellen Friedberg
Dr. and Mrs. Ben Friedman (Ruth)
Mr. and Mrs. Bruce Frieman (Susan)
Ms. Ethel Frieze
Mr. Vern Froelich
Ms. Frances Futch
Mr. and Mrs. James Gagliardi (Rhonda)
Mr. and Mrs. Lloyd Gamberg (Ellyn)
Ms. Margaret Garcia
Mr. and Mrs. Stanley Garnett, II (Carol)
Mr. and Mrs. Randy Geffon (Miranda)
Ms. Laurel Geise
Mr. and Mrs. Anthony Gentile
  (Francesca)
Mr. and Mrs. David George (Marlene)
Mr. and Mrs. Thomas George (Theresa)
Mr. and Mrs. Larry Gerahian (Dana)
Mr. and Mrs. B. Gray Gibbs (Bobbye)
Mr. and Mrs. L. Thomas Giblin (Chris)
Ms. Nancy Gibson
Mr. Wendy Giffin
Mr. and Mrs. Joel Giles (Anne)
Mr. and Mrs. Alec Gilholm (Berta)
Ms. Charlotte Gilmore
Mrs. Diane Giovanetti
Dr. and Mrs. Jorge Giroud (Darcy)
Mr. Fred Glass, Sr.
Ms. Karin P. Globus
Mr. and Mrs. Timothy Godwin
  (Maureen)
Mr. Will Goetz
Mr. and Mrs. Jeffrey Goodis (Heather)
Mr. and Mrs. Robert Gordon (Liz)
Mr. and Mrs. Ron Gorrell (Peggy)
Mr. Richard Goudey
Mr. and Mrs. John Gower (Suzanne)
Mr. and Mrs. Richard Graff (Harriet)
Mr. and Mrs. Doug Greenberg (Tammy)
Mr. and Mrs. Marcus Greene (Jennifer)
Mr. and Mrs. Lee Greene, III (Beverly)
Mr. and Mrs. March Greenstone
  (Roxann)
Ms. Cheryl Greenwood
Ms. Karin Griffin
Mr. William Griffith
Mr. Gerard Growney
Mr. Michael Grubbs
Mr. and Mrs. Trevor Grubbs (Claire)
Ms. Nyjola Grybauskas
Mr. and Mrs. Bob Guckenberger (Kathy)
Mr. and Mrs. Ken Guckenberger (Kathy)
Dr. and Mrs. Frederick Guerrier
  (Marlene)
Mr. and Mrs. Frederick Guest, II (Carole)
Ms. Donna Guillaume and Edward
  Kidston
Mr. and Mrs. Robert Guy (Carol)
Mr. and Mrs. Stefan Haberer (Elizabeth)
Mr. and Mrs. Robert Haddad (Susan)
Ms. Terry Hagstrom
Ms. Royce Haiman
Mr. and Mrs. Charles Hall (Anne)
Mr. Frank Hall
Mr. and Mrs. Karen Hamm (William)
Mr. and Mrs. John Handel (Gail)
Mr. and Mrs. Ted Hands (Sue)
Mr. Bert Hardesty
Mr. Robert Hargrove
Mr. Larry Harley and Jenny Cheek
Mr. and Mrs. Richard Harris (Patricia)
Mrs. Mary Harris Moeller
Mr. James Hartley
Mr. John D. Hartman (Gail McCauley)
Mr. and Mrs. Neil Hartney (Jaleen)
Dr. John Harvey
Mr. Dan Harvey, Jr.

Mr. and Mrs. Daniel Harvey, Sr. (Harriet)
Ms. Carol Haskitt
Mr. Harold Haskitt, Jr.
Mr. and Mrs. Bob Hastings (Onnie)
Mr. and Mrs. Michael Hastings (Jane)
Mr. and Mrs. Billy Hatcher (Karen)
Mr. and Mrs. Thomas Hatton (Pamela)
Mr. and Mrs. William Haueisen (Janice)
Mr. J. Tim Hawkins
Ms. Peggy Hawkins
Mr. and Mrs. Von Hayes (Stephanie)
Mr. Brett Hayman
Mr. Donald Haynie and Carole Oldham
Dr. and Mrs. Robert Heath (Eleanor)
Dr. and Mrs. Brian Hedrick (Lynn)
Mr. Clint Hege (Lew)
Ms. Sue Heichlinger
Mr. Terry Heidenreich
Mr. N. Hadley Heindel, Jr.
Mr. and Mrs. Rudy Heitler (Doris)
Mr. and Mrs. Charles Hellier (Joanne)
Mr. and Mrs. C. Blair Hennessey (Mitzi)
Mr. Thomas Hennessy
Mr. and Mrs. Alan Henry (Marilyn)
Ms. Eleanor Henry
Dr. James Henry
Mr. and Mrs. Michael Heraty (Mary Kay)
Mr. and Mrs. Ronald Hersch (Martha)
Mr. and Mrs. David Hicks (Linda)
Mr. and Mrs. John Higgins (Robin)
Mr. L avid Hill
Mr. and Mrs. Kevin Hirsch (Linda)
Mr. and Mrs. Stephen Hlas (Henny)
Mr. William Hoel
Mr. and Mrs. Gerry Hogan (Cathy)
Mr. and Mrs. G. C. Holland (Addie)
Mr. and Mrs. Troy Holland (Judy)
Ms. Carole Holsonback
Dr. and Mrs. William Holsonback (Gina)
Mr. and Mrs. Jeff Holzerland (Lisa)
Mr. Edward Hombordy (Nancy Gorman)
Mr. Peter Hooper
Col. Beverly Hoot
Ms. Diana Hoover
Mr. Harry Hope
Ms. Melinda Hopper
Mr. and Mrs. Greg Horn (Laura)
Mr. and Mrs. Terrence Hornsby (Laura)
Mrs. Marcia Horowitz and Dr. Erwin
  Horowitz
Mr. and Mrs. William Hough (Hazel)
Mr. and Mrs. W. Robb Hough, Jr.
  (Susan)
Mr. and Mrs. Paul Houlihan (Lori)
Mr. Joe Houlton and Dr. Mimi Houlton
Dr. Paul Hounchell
Ms. Cathy Howard
Mr. and Mrs. Jeffrey Howells (Mary-
  Ellen)
Ms. Terry Hubener
Mr. and Mrs. Jefrey Hudgins (Karen)
Mr. and Mrs. James Hulen (Hilde)
Mr. and Mrs. Randy Hunt (Wendy)
Mr. and Mrs. Neil Hurst (Karen)
Mr. Richard Hutchins
Mr. and Mrs. Anthony Ibarguen (Susan)
Mr. Eric Ingebritsen
Mr. and Mrs. Casey Ingram, III
  (Elisabeth)
Mr. and Mrs. Ian F. Irwin (Jean G.)
Ms. Jean Irwin
Mr. and Mrs. Charles Jackson, Jr. (Sally)
Dr. Geraldine Jacobson and Dr. Patrick
  Thomas
Mr. and Mrs. Todd Jakelis
Mr. and Mrs. William James (Janice)

Col. and Mrs. Charles James, Jr. (Cathy)
Mr. and Mrs. Frederick Javidi (Susan)
Mr. and Mrs. Tim Jesaitis (Susan)
Mr. J. Douglas Jester
Ms. Carol Jockers
Mr. and Mrs. David Johnson (Lynn)
Dr. and Mrs. David Johnson (Caryle)
Mr. and Mrs. Don Johnson (Marilyn)
Mr. and Mrs. James Johnson (Rosemary)
Mr. and Mrs. Scott Johnston (Pattie)
Mr. and Mrs. W. Richard Johnston
    (Linda)
Mr. George Jones
Ms. Judith Jourdan
Mr. and Mrs. Sie Kamide (Ruth)
Mr. Dean Karikas
Ms. Diane Keane
Mr. and Mrs. Joseph Keegan (Sharon)
Dr. and Mrs. William Keeler, III (Mary
    Louise)
Mr. and Mrs. Allen Keesler, Jr. (Sarah)
Mr. and Mrs. G. W. Keller (Sharon)
Mr. and Mrs. Peter Kelly (Joan)
Mr. and Mrs. Kevin Kelso (Amy)
Mr. and Mrs. Michael Kelzer (Kathleen)
Mr. Brian Kennelly and Gretchen Minor
Mr. Timothy Kennelly
Mr. and Mrs. William Kent (Elizabeth)
Mr. Charles Kessock
Mr. and Mrs. Wade Key (Susan)
Mr. and Mrs. John Kiernan (Jane)
Mr. and Mrs. Michael Kiernan (Darla)
Mr. and Mrs. Matt Kilgroe (Carrie)
Mr. and Mrs. Tim Killam (Linda)
Dr. and Mrs. John Killinen (Gertraud)
Mr. and Mrs. Robert Kindig (Marjorie)
Mr. and Mrs. Richard Kiracofe (Lonnie)
Mr. and Mrs. Robert Kirby (Jane)
Ms. Barbara Kirk
Mr. and Mrs. George Knight (Cheryl)
Mr. and Mrs. Webster Knight (Barbara)
Mr. and Mrs. Richard Knipe (Sue)
Dr. and Mrs. Stephen Kobernick
    (Debbie)
Mrs. Johanna Koch
Mr. and Mrs. Robert Koch (Judith)
Mr. and Mrs. Werner Koester (Martha)
Mr. and Mrs. Doug Kohlhepp (Jackie)
Mr. and Mrs. Erwin Koltay
Mr. and Mrs. John Kool (Sharon)
Mr. and Mrs. Donald Korns (Debra)
Mr. and Mrs. Richard Korpan (Patricia)
Drs. James Kosydar and Michelle Albers
Mr. and Mrs. Tom Kowenhoven (Kathy)
Mr. and Mrs. Mickey Kramer, Sr.
    (Rebecca)
Mr. Glenn Kranzow
Mr. and Mrs. Patrick Kraujalis (Debbie)
Dr. and Mrs. James Krause (Jean)
Mrs. Carole Krayer and A. C. Krayer
Dr. and Mrs. Robert Kropp (Teresa)
Mr. and Mrs. Ford Kyes (Barbara)
Mr. Jon LaBudde and Claudia Bridgeford
Mr. and Mrs. Gerald Labie (Amy)
Mr. and Mrs. John Lake (Katharine)
Mr. and Mrs. Charles LaMar (Cheryl)
Mr. and Mrs. Clark Lambert (Barbara)
Mr. and Mrs. Carl Lambrecht (Lee Ann)
Mr. Dean Lampe
Mr. and Mrs. James Landers (Angela)
Mr. and Mrs. Jeff Lane (Barbara)

Dr. and Mrs. James LaPolla (Leslie)
Mr. and Mrs. Jeffrey Larson (Dee Ann)
Ms. Lorie Larson
Mr. and Mrs. Mark Larson (Joy)
Mr. Walter Larson
Dr. George Lasche
Ms. Ruth Latimer
Mr. and Mrs. Joseph Laughlin (Colleen)
Mr. Steven Lavely
Mr. Jerald Lavin (Kelley)
Mr. and Mrs. Richard Lazzara (Debbie)
Mr. S. Brad Lazzara
Mr. and Mrs. Darryl LeClair (Melissa)
Mr. and Mrs. John Lee (Dorothea)
Mr. and Mrs. Marion Lee (Carol)
Mr. and Mrs. Mitchell Lee (Linda)
Ms. Jane Ann Lees and Ronald Lee
Mr. and Mrs. Edward Legendre (Gina)
Dr. Karen Lenhart
Mr. and Mrs. Richard Leverone (Joanne)
Dr. and Mrs. Myles Levitt (Pamela)
Ms. Kathryn Lewis
Mr. and Mrs. Sam Lewis (Suzette)
Ms. Linda Linardos
Mr. Carl Lindell, Jr.
Mr. and Mrs. Tony Linguanti, Jr. (Debra)
Mr. Jack Logan, Jr.
Mr. and Mrs. John Long (Cathy)
Ms. Sarah Lonquist
Mr. John Lubbe
Mr. and Mrs. Joseph Lucas (Marjorie)
Mr. and Mrs. James Luckey (Libby)
Dr. and Mrs. Bernard Ludes (Miriam)
Mr. Michael Lynch
Mr. and Mrs. William Lynch (Beth)
Mr. and Mrs. Claude Macari (Mary)
Mr. and Mrs. Frederick MacFawn, III
Mr. and Mrs. Charles Mackey
Mr. and Mrs. Carlen Maddux (Martha)
Mr. and Mrs. Michael Maguire (Julie)
Mr. and Mrs. Mark Mahaffey (Marianne)
Mr. and Mrs. Bill Maher (Mary Jo)
Mr. and Mrs. Timothy Main (Jayma)
Mr. and Mrs. Laura Mallon (Douglas)
Mr. and Mrs. Mark Mandula (Kathy)
Mr. and Mrs. James Mann (S. Anne)
Rev. and Mrs. Timothy Mann (Ann)
Mr. Tim Marcum
Dr. and Mrs. Jeffrey Marder (Jill)
Ambas. Jamsheed Marker (Arnaz)
Mr. and Mrs. Christopher Marois
    (Michele)
Dr. and Mrs. Richard Martinez (Peggy)
Mr. and Mrs. Wendel Martinkovic
    (Marie)
Mr. and Mrs. Lee Martino (Jackie)
Mr. and Mrs. Ralph Martino (Grace)
Mr. Donald Mason
Dr. and Mrs. James Mason (Shirley)
Mr. and Mrs. Ronald Mason (Patricia)
Ms. Celma Mastry
Mr. and Mrs. Richard Mastry (Denise)
Mr. and Mrs. Paul Matecki (Kathleen)
Mr. and Mrs. Donald Mathias (Linda)
Mr. and Mrs. Gray Mattern (Georgia)
Mr. and Mrs. Gregory Matthews
    (Kathleen)
Mr. and Mrs. David Matthies (JoAnn)
Mr. and Mrs. Jerry Matus (Lin)
Mr. Steven McAuliffe (Rachel)
Mr. and Mrs. Sean McCall, Jr. (Allison)
Mr. and Mrs. Denise McCanless (Mike)
Mr. and Mrs. Terence McCarthy (Ginny)
Mr. and Mrs. Thomas McClelland
    (Dona)
Mr. and Mrs. Dick McClure (Rebecca)

Dr. and Mrs. Jorge McCormack (Celia)
Ms. Cynthia McCormick
Mr. and Mrs. Frederic McCoy (Barbara)
Ms. Dorothy McCuish
Ms. Janette McCurley
Mr. Donald McDonald
Mr. and Mrs. Emery McDonough
    (LeeAnne)
Mr. and Mrs. Kenneth McDowell (Amy)
Mr. and Mrs. Joseph McEwen (Aila)
Ms. Catherine McGarry
Ms. Julia McGinty
Mr. and Mrs. Thomas McGowan
    (Marilyn)
Mr. and Mrs. Barry McIntosh (Patricia)
Ms. Elizabeth McIntyre
Mr. and Mrs. Craig McLaughlin (Millie)
Dr. and Mrs. John McLemore (Laura)
Mr. and Mrs. William McMasters (Dixie)
Mr. and Mrs. Michael McNally (Theresa)
Mr. and Mrs. Terrance McNamara
    (Laurie)
Dr. and Mrs. Thomas McNeill (Shannon)
Mr. and Mrs. William McQueen (Maria)
Mrs. Tish McQuillen
Mr. and Mrs. David Meehan (Lisa)
Mrs. Fanitsa Meehan
Mr. Don Mehan
Mr. and Mrs. Fred Mein (Adel)
Mr. and Mrs. Robert Melby (Jane)
Mr. and Mrs. Robert G. Menke (Amy)
Mr. and Mrs. Robert M. Menke (Jan)
Mr. and Mrs. Peter Metcalfe (Denise)
Mr. and Mrs. Peter Metzger (Andrea)
Mr. Stephen Michaud
Mr. Jonathan Micocci
Mr. John Migliorelli
Mr. Emil Miller
Mr. and Mrs. Jay Miller (Jamielove)
Dr. and Mrs. Robert Miller (Patricia)
Ms. Terese Miller
Mr. and Mrs. Richard Minck (Helen)
Mr. Michael Mitchell
Mr. and Mrs. Thomas Mitchell
    (Catherine)
Mr. and Mrs. Thomas Money (Wendy)
Mr. and Mrs. John Montanari (Pamela)
Ms. Linda Moore
Mr. and Mrs. William Morean (Kelly)
Mr. and Mrs. Davenport Mosby (Glenn)
Mr. and Mrs. Randy Moss (Cathy)
Mr. and Mrs. Alan Mossberg (Jayne)
Ms. Gail Moyer
Mr. John Muchard
Mr. James Mulchay
Mr. John Mullaney
Mr. and Mrs. Sean Mulligan, III (Cyndi)
Mr. and Mrs. Thomas Murphy (Michelle)
Dr. and Mrs. David Murray (Linda)
Ms. Dede Murtagh
Mr. Don Myette
Ms. Joyce Nader and Adrian Cuarta
Mr. and Mrs. Robert Nader
Dr. and Mrs. Jeffrey Nadler (Constance
    Price)
Mr. and Mrs. Robert Nagel (Mary Anne)
Mr. and Mrs. James Nagelsen (Donna)
Mr. Raymond Naimoli
Mr. and Mrs. Vincent Naimoli (Linda)
Dr. Anthony Napolitano
Mr. and Mrs. George Naruns, D.C.
    (Peggy)
Dr. and Mrs. Michael Nauert (Jodell)
Mr. and Mrs. Jim Neader (Michelle)
Mr. and Mrs. Kalju Nekvasil (Johanna)
Mr. and Mrs. Richard Nelson (Carolyn)

Dr. and Mrs. Jeffrey Neustadt (Susan)
Mr. and Mrs. Patricia Newman (Dan)
Mr. and Mrs. Larry Newsome (Bettye)
Mr. and Mrs. Robert Newton, Jr. (Lynne)
Mr. and Mrs. Stephen Nichols (Margaret)
Mr. and Mrs. Michael Nicholson (Larise)
Dr. and Mrs. Russell Norris (Martha)
Mr. and Mrs. Anthony Norungolo (Anne
    Sullivan)
Mr. Chris Novilla
Mr. and Mrs. Michael O'Brien (Dianne)
Mr. Thomas O'Daniel
Mr. and Mrs. George Off (Tara)
Mr. and Mrs. Joe O'Grady (Donna)
Mr. Gregory O'Keeffe (Linda)
Mrs. Diane Oldja (John)
Mr. and Mrs. Preben Olesen (Darla)
Judge and Mrs. David O'Neil (Barbara)
Dr. and Mrs. Gary Onik (Janet)
Dr. and Mrs. Peter Orobello (Jill)
Mr. and Mrs. Philip Orsino (Helen)
Mr. Kurt Ott
Mr. and Mrs. Norm Ott, Jr. (Ruth Ann)
Ms. Mary Lou Pahigian
Mr. and Mrs. Jack Painter (Donna)
Ms. Margaret Painter
Mr. and Mrs. Bruce Pardy (Cynthia)
Mr. and Mrs. John Park (Pepita)
Mr. and Mrs. Dale Parker (Erin)
Mr. and Mrs. Jeffrey Parker (Kathryn)
Mr. and Mrs. Tom Parsley (Betty)
Mr. Tom Parsley
Mr. and Mrs. Ed Parsley, Sr.
Mr. and Mrs. Charlie Parsons (Frances)
Mr. Gorgon Parsons
Mr. and Mrs. Ray Pasqualone (Kristina)
Mr. and Mrs. Yogesh Pathak (Shobhna)
Ms. Pamela Patterson
Dr. Thomas Paulantonio
Mr. and Mrs. Ira Pearson (Cheryl)
Mr. and Mrs. Bert Perozzi (Robin)
Mr. and Mrs. John Petagna (Alice)
Mr. Edward Peters
Mr. and Mrs. Stephen Peters (Lisa)
Ms. Mandy Peterson
Mr. and Mrs. Charles Philips (Barbara)
Dr. Joseph Pilkington
Mr. Michael Piper
Mr. and Mrs. Richard Pless (Lynn)
Mr. and Mrs. John Pontzer (Carolyn)
Mr. and Mrs. David A. Porter (Kathleen)
Mr. Warren Potenberg
Mr. and Mrs. Robert Potter (Mary)
Mr. and Mrs. Richard Powers (Cary)
Mr. and Mrs. Robert Powers, Jr.
    (Maureen)
Mr. and Mrs. Robert (Reed) Powers, Jr.
    (Maureen)
Ms. Sally Poynter
Ms. Jean Prina
Mr. and Mrs. John Prosser (Kathi)
Mr. E. Wilson Purdy
Mr. and Mrs. Cary Putrino (Joan)
Dr. Victoria Quezon
Mr. and Mrs. Farris Rahall (Victoria)
Mr. George Rahdert
Mr. and Mrs. Eduardo Raheb (Dora)
Mr. Albert Rawlins
Col. and Mrs. Richard Raymond (Clare)
Mr. and Mrs. Steen Raymund (Sonia)
Mr. and Mrs. Fred Razook (Gail)
Mr. Wayne Read
Mr. Terrill Reeb
Mr. and Mrs. Tom Reed (Connie Wilson)
Mr. and Mrs. James Reichert (Sandra)
Dr. Michael Reilly

Mr. and Mrs. Paul Reilly (Sheila)
Mr. and Mrs. Paul Renker (Lynda)
Mr. and Mrs. Joseph Reppert (Colleen)
Mr. and Mrs. Larry Rhum (Debra)
Mr. and Mrs. Edward Richardson
   (Theresa)
Mr. and Mrs. Joseph Richardson (Karen)
Mr. deWayne Richey
Ms. Sherri Richey
Mr. and Mrs. Jeffrey Ritch (Lane)
Ms. Judith Roales
Mr. and Mrs. Michael Robbins (Penny
   Lynn)
Ms. Evelyn Roberts
Mr. James Roberts
Mr. and Mrs. Pryor Robertson (Helga)
Mr. and Mrs. R. Clarke Robinson
   (Diane)
Mr. John Rogers
Dr. and Mrs. Raymond Rogowski
   (Dorothy)
Mr. and Mrs. Lawrence Rooney (Loretta)
Mr. and Mrs. Daniel Rosefelt (Michele)
Dr. and Mrs. Andrew Rosenthal (Sandra)
Mr. James Rossi
Ms. Dolly Rote
Dr. and Mrs. James Rothermel (Midge)
Dr. Harry Rothwell, Jr.
Dr. and Mrs. Scott Rubin (Haris Lender-
   Rubin)
Mr. and Mrs. Rhodes Rucker (Marianne)
Mr. Lee Rudolph
Mrs. Lola Ruggiero
Ms. Aimee Russell
Mr. Harold Russell
Mr. and Mrs. J. C. Russell (Carol)
Mr. and Mrs. William Russo, Jr. (Terry
   Halstrom)
Mr. and Mrs. Dave Ruth (Bonnie)
Ms. Nancy Rutland
Mr. and Mrs. Mark Rutledge (Mandy)
Ms. Dorothy Sable
Mr. and Mrs. Bruce Sadler (Mary)
Ms. Katherine Safford
Dr. and Mrs. Kenneth Safko (Emily)
Mr. and Mrs. Ronald Salamone
   (Elizabeth)
Mr. and Mrs. Eino Salo (Mary)
Dr. and Mrs. Albert Saltiel (Deborah)
Mr. and Mrs. Mark Samardich (Lynn)
Mr. and Mrs. Jared Samon (Melanie)
Dr. and Mrs. Bernt Sanders (Ursula)
Mr. Robert Sanderson
Mr. and Mrs. Steven Sanet (Judi)
Mrs. Barbara Sansone (Terry Collins)
Ms. Gale Santacreu
Mr. and Mrs. Stephen Sargent (Julie)
Mr. and Mrs. William Saron (Carole)
Mr. and Mrs. Donald Saunders, II
   (Merritt)
Mr. and Mrs. Drew Sauter (Lee)
Mr. Neil Savage
Mr. and Mrs. Richard Scanlon (Leslie)
Mr. Millard Schindler
Mr. Joseph Schmerge (Laura)
Mr. and Mrs. Donald Schmidt (Yanina)
Dr. and Mrs. Robert Schreiber (Garnet)
Dr. F. William Schroeder
Ms. Debbie Schultz
Mr. and Mrs. Neal Schwartz (Lisa)
   Ms. Janet Schweitzer
Mr. and Mrs. Lee Scott (Margaret)
Ms. Mary Scribner
Mr. and Mrs. John Seaman (Bettye)
Mr. and Mrs. Doran Seaquist (Doris)

Mr. and Mrs. Subhash Shah (Kokila)
Dr. and Mrs. Gilbert Shamas (Anne)
Mr. Morris Shapero
Mr. William Sharrow
Mr. and Mrs. Ronald Shashy (Alice)
Mr. Jazz Shasteen
Mr. Thomas Shelton
Dr. and Mrs. Robert Sheppard (Ina)
Mr. and Mrs. Stephen Sherrill (Kerry)
Mr. and Mrs. Frank Shields (Lisette)
Mr. and Mrs. Neil Shoaf (Janet)
Mr. Robert Shoemaker
Mr. and Mrs. Vincent Shook (Teri)
Dr. and Mrs. Alan Shoopak (Carol)
Mr. Byron Shouppe
Mr. Robert Siclari
Ms. Janene Silver
Mr. James Sirmons
Mr. and Mrs. Robert Siver (Nancy)
Ms. Patricia Skelton
Mr. and Mrs. Roy Smay (Dottie)
Mr. and Mrs. Brian Smith (Constance)
Mr. and Mrs. David Smith (Mary Chris)
Mr. and Mrs. Derwin Smith (Marilyn)
Mr. and Mrs. John Smith (Sandra)
Ms. Sandra Smith
Mr. and Mrs. E. W. Smith, III (Margaret)
Mr. and Mrs. E. W. Smith (Barbara)
Ms. Lisa Smithson
Ms. Shantell Smithson
Dr. and Mrs. Curtis Songster (Julie)
Mr. and Mrs. William Specht (Laurel)
Mr. and Mrs. Chris Spiller (Melinda)
Mr. W. Gordon Spoor (Virginia)
Mr. and Mrs. Darrell Springer (Paulee)
Dr. Joseph Springle (Karen Rosenthal)
Mr. Fernand St. Germain
Mr. and Mrs. Richard Stang (Elizabeth)
Mr. and Mrs. Fred Stansberry (Sheila
   Thurmond)
Ms. Carla Stanton
Dr. Jennifer Steel
Mr. and Mrs. Henry Stein (Marty)
Mr. and Mrs. Jack Stein (Kathleen)
Mr. and Mrs. Nelson Steiner (Lynne)
Mr. and Mrs. Robert Steiner (Suzan)
Mr. and Mrs. Paul Steinhauser (Carolyn)
Mr. and Mrs. Christopher Steinocher
   (Julian)
Mrs. Doris Anne Stephens
Mr. and Mrs. Robert Stewart (Carol)
Mr. and Mrs. Scott Stewart (Irene
   Haggar)
Mr. and Mrs. Peyton Stone (Betty)
Mr. and Mrs. John Stoner (Linda)
Ms. Mary Stovall
Mr. and Mrs. Jack Strauser (Jean)
Mr. and Mrs. Robert Strickland (Lynn)
Mr. and Mrs. Thomas Strickland, Sr.
   (Bonnie)
Mr. and Mrs. Don Strobel (Neverne)
Mr. and Mrs. J. Mark Stroud (Celeste)
Mr. and Mrs. Robert Stuart (Huldah)
Mr. Kristopher Swayze
Ms. Mary Sweeney
Dr. and Mrs. Robert Swiggett, Jr. (Mary
   Joan)
Mr. Laszlo I. Szerenyi
Mr. and Mrs. Thomas Szilage, Sr. (Anne)
Mr. and Mrs. Thomas Taggart (Susan)
Dr. and Mrs. Terry Tanner (Lynn)
Mr. and Mrs. Paul Tash (Karyn)
Dr. and Mrs. Hilt Tatum, III (Scarlett)
Ms. Helen Taulman
Mr. and Mrs. John Terlip (Beth)

Mr. and Mrs. Edward Thoenes (Melanie)
Mr. and Mrs. Bill Thomas (Trish)
Ms. Cary Bond Thomas
Mr. and Mrs. Grank Thompson (Maria)
Mr. and Mrs. Graham Thompson (Ellen)
Mr. James Thompson
Mr. and Mrs. James Thompson (Audrey)
Mr. and Mrs. James Thompson, Jr.
   (Alice)
Ms. Betty Thornhill
Mr. and Mrs. Bob Timberlake (Beth)
Mr. and Mrs. Bruce Titus (Jane)
Mr. and Mrs. John Toppe (Melanie)
Mr. Helen Torres
Lt. Col. Jean Trask
Mr. and Mrs. Robert Traviesa (Lynn)
Mr. and Mrs. Tony Traviesa (Linda)
Mr. and Mrs. Thomas Tremaine (Leyla)
Mr. and Mrs. Eric Tridas (Ann)
Dr. James Truax
Mr. and Mrs. Kiefer Tucker (Miriam)
Ms. Leigh Ann Tucker
Mr. and Mrs. Gerald Tuite (Susan)
Ms. Anneliese Tuns and Ulrich Koj
Mr. and Mrs. Clyde Turner (Debbie)
Ms. Sara Turner
Mr. Edward Twyford, III
Mr. and Mrs. Dean Tyler (Donna)
Mr. Brent Tynan
Mr. and Mrs. Steve Uebel (Rosemary)
Ms. Mona Ulen
Ms. Lisa Ulrich
Dr. and Mrs. Ambrose Updegraff
   (Ramona)
Dr. and Mrs. Stephen Updegraff
   (Elizabeth)
Ms. Liliane Vaden
Dr. Hugh van Gelder
Mr. and Mrs. Peter Van Scoik (Unissa)
Mr. and Mrs. Russell Van Zandt (Judith)
Drs. Glenn and Mimi Vaughn
Mr. and Mrs. Rick Vaughn
Mr. and Mrs. Michael Veeck (Elizabeth)
Mr. and Mrs. John Venable (Catherine)
Mr. and Mrs. Ann Vickstrom (Dan)
Mr. and Mrs. Robert Vincent (Alice)
Mr. Joe Vitello, Jr.
Mr. and Mrs. Donald Volpe (Julie)
Mr. and Mrs. Dean Von Pusch (Rita)
Dr. Marcia Wagaman
Mr. and Mrs. David Wagner (Judi)
Mr. William Waite
Mr. Barry Wall
Mr. Karl Wall
Mr. and Mrs. Andrew Wallace (Wendy)
Mr. and Mrs. Thomas Wallace (Susan)
Mr. and Mrs. William Wallace (Sally)
Mr. and Mrs. Timothy Walsh (R.
   Rodriguez-Walsh)
Ms. R. Ann Walters
Mr. and Mrs. Les Wandler (Susan)
Mr. and Mrs. Richard E. Ware (Kelly)
Mr. and Mrs. Richard M. Ware (Maria)
Mr. Mark Warlaumont
Mr. and Mrs. Mark Waterbury (Sandra)
Mr. and Mrs. Scott Watson (Martha)
Ms. Frances Louise Weaver (Tom Stovall)
Mr. Vey Weaver
Mr. Arthur Weaver, Jr.
Mr. and Mrs. George Webb (Robin)
Gen. and Mrs. Hamilton Webb (Esther)
Mr. and Mrs. Douglas Weber (Eileen)
Mr. and Mrs. Ron Weidner (Linda)
Mr. and Mrs. Rudolph Weihe (Starr)
Dr. and Mrs. Richard Weinberger

(Gloria)
Mr. and Mrs. Conrad Weishaupt (Jill)
Ms. Judy Weitekamp
Mr. and Mrs. Harold Wells (Ann)
Mr. and Mrs. Peter Wells (Lisa)
Ms. Sandy Wells
Mr. and Mrs. Brad Wendkos (Susan)
Mr. and Mrs. Charles Weniger (Margaret)
Ms. Aramynta West
Ms. Danette Whalen (Michael Whalen)
Mr. and Mrs. Donald Wheeler (Patricia)
Mr. Whit Whitacre
Col. and Mrs. Billy White (T. J.)
Ms. Janet White
Mr. and Mrs. Jeff White (Carla)
Mr. Richard White
Mr. and Mrs. Robert White (Mollie)
Mr. Terry White
Mr. Robert Whiting
Mr. and Mrs. James Whittlesey (Judy)
Ms. Terry Wigginton
Mr. and Mrs. David Wilbanks (Judy)
Dr. Beverly Wilcher
Mr. Richard Wilkes
Mr. and Mrs. Roland Wilkinson, Jr.
   (Donna)
Mr. Charles Will, Jr.
Mr. and Mrs. Leo Willett, IV (Marci)
Mr. and Mrs. James Williams (Cynthia)
Ms. Julie Williams
Drs. Larry and Sarah Williams
Ms. Dorothy H. Wilson
Ms. Joyce Wilson
Ms. Margaret Wilson
Mr. Jeffrey Winkler (Dr. Ann Winkler)
Ms. Mary Margaret Winning
Mr. and Mrs. Richard Winning
Ms. Deborah Winters
Ms. Linda Wittman
Mr. and Mrs. Ted Wittner (Jean)
Prof. and Mrs. Ronald Witzel (Elisabeth)
Mr. and Mrs. Mark Wolfinger (Rochelle)
Mr. and Mrs. William Wollerscheid
   (Mimi)
Mr. Frank Womack
Mr. and Mrs. Emory Wood (Margaret)
Mr. James Wood, IV
Mr. John Woodruff
Mr. and Mrs. Tony Woods (Lois)
Ms. Virginia Workman
Mr. and Mrs. Patrick Wybrow (Dale)
Mr. and Mrs. Dennis Wynn (Jean)
Mr. and Mrs. Eugene Yennie (M. Kay)
Mr. and Mrs. Carlos Yepes (Beverly)
Mr. Ralph Ytterberg
Mr. and Mrs. Andy Zaccaria (Barbara)
Mr. and Mrs. Joseph Zagame (Jane)
Mr. Dane Zimring
Mr. and Mrs. Devin Zimring (Kathryn)
Ms. Lisa Zimring
Mr. and Mrs. Harry Zweifel (Heidi)

This list of Vinoy Club Members was
compiled in April of 1999.

Bibliography

Books

Open For The Season. Abbott, Karl P. Doubleday & Company,Inc., 1952, Garden City, New York.

A History of Florida. Tebeau, Charlton W. University of Miami (Fla.) Press, 1973, Miami, Florida.

St. Petersburg and The Florida Dream. Raymond Arsenault. 1996, by the Board of Regents of the State of Florida, the University Press of Florida.

St. Petersburg: Once Upon A Time, Memories of Places & People - 1890s to 1990s. Marth, Del R. and Martha J. Suwannee River Press, Branford, Florida, 1996.

Baseball in Florida. McCarthy, Kevin M. Pineapple Press, Inc., 1996.

World War II in Tampa Bay. de Quesada, Alejandro M. Arcadia Publishing, Charleston, South Carolina, 1997.

Magazine Articles

Tourist News, February 28, 1925.

Tourist News, August 15, 1925.

The Florida Historical Quarterly. Volume LXXIII, no. 1. July 1994.

Women and War: St. Petersburg Women During World War II by Ellen J. Babb, 43–61.

War and Peace on the Suncoast: A Photo Essay. Tampa Bay History. Volume 3, no. 2, Fall/Winter 1981.

Tampa Bay Life. September 1990. Profile of Frederick E. Guest II, by Gary Lantrip.

INDEX

ABOUT THE AUTHOR

Prudy Taylor Board is a native of Florida and a graduate of the University of Florida who has devoted much of her professional life to preserving the history of her beloved state.

As a freelance journalist and novelist, she has had more than a thousand articles published in national and regional magazines. She was a staff writer for the FORT MYERS NEWS PRESS, assignment editor and reporter for the CBS and NBC television affiliates in Fort Myers, managing editor of two regional magazines, LEE LIVING and HOME AND CONDO. She also edited THE FICTION WRITER, a magazine for writers distributed nationally.

Her first book, LEE COUNTY: A PICTORIAL HISTORY, was published by the Donning Company/Publishers in 1985. Her novels, THE VOW AND BLOOD LEGACY, were published in 1989 by Leisure Books and PocketBooks. Donning published her most recent books—PAGES FROM THE PAST: A PICTORIAL RETROSPECTIVE OF LEE COUNTY, FLORIDA; HISTORIC FORT MYERS, FL; VENICE (FL) THROUGH THE YEARS; THE BELLEVIEW MIDO HOTEL; A CENTURY OF HOSPITALITY, and MENDING MINDS, HEALING HEARTS: THE HISTORY OF THE FLORIDA SHERIFFS YOUTH RANCHES. Donning recently contracted with Board to write the history of Barry University in Miami, FL.

Board has taught writing courses in Fort Myers, Naples and Delray Beach, FL and at Edison Community College in Lee County, FL. She lectures frequently at writers' conferences around the country. She now lives in Delray Beach.

W SPA BEACH AND VINOY PARK HOTEL, ST. PE